Peace at Heart

An Oregon Country Life

Barbara Drake

Oregon State University Press
Corvallis

The paper in this book meets the guidelines for permanence and durability of the Committee on Production Guidelines for Book Longevity of the Council on Library Resources and the minimum requirements of the American National Standard for Permanence of Paper for Printed Library Materials Z39.48-1984.

Library of Congress Cataloging-in-Publication Data
Drake, Barbara.
    Peace at Heart : an Oregon country life / Barbara Drake.
        p. cm.
    ISBN 0-87071-455-4 (alk paper)
    1. Country life—Oregon—Willamette River Valley. 2. Drake, Barbara. 3. Willamette River Valley (Or.)—Social life and customs. 4. Willamette River Valley (Or.)—Biography. I. Title.
    F882.W6D73 1998
    979.53—dc21   98-23928
                                                              CIP

Oregon State University Press
101 Waldo Hall
Corvallis OR 97331-6407
541-737-3166 •fax 541-737-3170
osu.orst.edu/dept/press

To Eben and Griffin.
May you grow up in a world of peace, joy,
and natural beauty.

With loving appreciation to
William Beckman, the hero of this book.

Contents

Preface

⊕

In 1987, when we moved to the country, I felt as if I were returning to something. But it was a "return" to where I'd never been. Before I can remember, during the first two years of my life, my parents lived on a sheep farm in Kansas. I was familiar with the family mythology—the huge flocks of sheep; Fannie, our sable border collie; Mary and Joe Littlebird, the Native American couple who camped on our farm when they brought their greyhounds to the races and who gave me a pair of baby-sized, beaded moccasins as a birth gift; the wild ducks on the river; "Sweet Pea," the hired man; the alfalfa fields; my grandfather on horseback with his rifle slung on the saddle—but my grandfather died when I was only six months old, and my conscious memory begins later on, in the West, after we left Kansas.

Nevertheless, when my husband Bill and I moved to the farm, there was a feeling of having come full circle. I recognized the sweet smell of alfalfa and sheep's wool as if I'd been born in a barn. At the same time, I was gifted with that sharpening of senses that comes when things are wholly new and unfamiliar. It was in that state of newness that I began to write the essays which make up this book. I didn't know where they would lead, but the process of writing is often one of recognition. As one subject or event after another caught my attention and begged to be recorded, I realized that there were patterns in those events that were older, even, than the Kansas farm. Things I had "known" all my life suddenly became more real when I encountered them day by day.

Though I had a religious upbringing; and though I had studied regeneration myths in college literature classes and had read Frazer and Weston; and though I had even given birth three times; been party to weddings, baptisms, and rites for the dead; crossed the Atlantic in spring storms and was nearly lost at sea; and once, even, had my house struck by lightning; until we moved to the farm, it now seems to me, there was some narrow film between myself and the archetype.

I am not without imagination. Like most people, I assume, I have looked up at the stars, thought of their distance and immensity, and felt, with heart-stopping suddenness, as if I were falling out of my body. I have floated in rivers on warm days in late summer and lost track of the boundaries of self. I have had moments of spiritual dislocation that I can describe only as feelings of unreality.

On the farm, to the contrary, reality suddenly fell into place.

Ten years went by. I became used to birthing lambs and drinking home-grown wine. The hawks returned to their nests each spring. Life bloomed after the dead of winter. It seemed I knew every wild flower on the place.

Then, last December, my six-month-old grandbaby arrived for his first Christmas visit. He is a relaxed and happy baby, quick to observe and take in life's experiences.

"I'm going to show him the sheep," I told my daughter. We went to the barn, Eben riding my arm with an alert and expectant air. It was late in the afternoon and the barn was dim inside. I called the sheep and tossed some alfalfa into the feed bin. At first, Eben didn't seem to notice them. Then, suddenly, he saw them. He let out a scream of sheer terror.

We ran from the barn as if from the Medusa.

I hugged and comforted him and his good humor soon returned. Even as I felt protective pity and regret for his fear, I also had a hard time not laughing because his reaction so surprised me. And yet I saw, in that brief second of terror, this baby's own view of the animals. I saw the rams' great hairy faces, their growth of winter wool hanging like thick moss, their gleaming golden eyes with the horizontal slits. I saw their mouths open and the long wet tongues protruding as they bellowed, sending steam and a stench of fermenting hay onto the cold winter air. In that moment I remembered the Minotaur, Sasquatch, and a figure I'd seen on a red and black Greek vase, a shaggy-headed goat man dancing.

Throughout history, human beings have been trying to figure out their relationship to, their place in, the animal world. Are we wholly apart from them? Are we of them? Of course Eben screamed. He was only six months old and had lived all his life so far with his parents in a downtown Seattle apartment. Aside from "Brother," my daughter's fat old cat, Eben had not had a close-up experience with animals. When they appeared so suddenly, the rams must have seemed like monsters, underworld beings that didn't fit the paradigm of human city life. Suddenly he had encountered the "others," and they were large and hairy and loud. I felt bad that I had shown him the sheep without ceremony, without adequate preparation.

We returned to the house for comfort among relatives, but later, after a certain amount of planning and discussion, we made another excursion to the barn. His mother came along. This time he was curious, peeping wide-eyed around the door of the barn and even putting out his hand to touch the head of a sheep at the railing, like a sort of communicant, or perhaps he was the one giving the blessing, though he pulled his hand back quickly and was cautious about the whole event. It seemed he was not going to be afraid of them after all.

And for myself, I was grateful to Eben for reminding me to be impressed by the sheep, to look at them, as all of nature, with not a little awe.

I think it is a privilege to live so familiarly with animals. Of course, sometimes when I am feeding the sheep their alfalfa or carrying the blue basin freshly filled with water for the dogs, when I am going out to the chicken pen with a pan full of melon rinds or scattering a bucket of grain, when I am giving the cats their tiny fishy pellets of food, I say to myself: "Look at me: I've grown up to be the servant of animals!" Then I picture myself as a kind of minion in humble garments bringing the animals their feed, or an acolyte at some ancient service. But it's not a bad kind of servitude, and we humans are part of the cycle and extract our commission.

It is interesting, living in the country. Animals and plants, seasons and weather, all make regular demands on our attention. In early spring, when the grape vines still look like dead sticks, there is a definite tension as we wait for "bud break," the event which signals that the vines are alive and are going to begin to grow and make fruit again. In the fall, when the grass is yellow and the dry leaves wither on the vines, looking like peeling skin or the soft wings of sleeping bats, we harvest ripe grapes with gratitude and celebrate with wine from preceding years.

We have a lot of daffodils but I like to add a few new bulbs every October, just in case. As I plant them, invariably there are flocks of migratory geese flying over, flocks I would miss if I were inside doing something else. This ceremony of planting bulbs in autumn is a commitment to some future beauty, the continuation of life whether the individual gardener returns or not. Good is bound to come from it. Perhaps there should be a national holiday.

In the country, we are intensely aware of the weather, and where the farm is situated, on a ridge with views both east and west, we get a clear view of each day's arriving and departing light. From the bedroom, we have only to open our eyes to see the sun rising over Chehalem ridge. In the evening we move toward the western side of the place and watch the sun go down. We also look to the west for fogs and rainstorms coming over the Coast Range as we look to the east for thunderheads and high pressure. The seasonal movements of the sun from north to south and back again are clear as figures on a calendar. I have visited Stonehenge and Avebury in southern England and Newgrange in Ireland. Seeing those Neolithic monuments, I have thought: well, of course. I may not erect stones to the purpose, but I know that on the spring equinox the sun will set almost exactly at the peak of Trask Mountain as seen from my front porch.

In the ten years we have lived on Lilac Hill, there have been many family events tied intimately with the landscape. We celebrated a wedding in the upper oak grove. Streamers of purple and white satin flickered in the September breeze and tangled with the oak branches as a son and daughter-in-law said their vows. Lamb and wine, potato salad, deviled eggs, fresh vegetables, all from the farm, were set out on the banquet table.

Two new babies, Eben and Griffin, have been welcomed into the family and have made their first ceremonial visits to the farm. Older grandchildren—Gwen, Manuel, and Zachary—have learned the routine of feeding apples to the sheep, filling the chicken feeder, gathering eggs. All of them have slept under blankets made from our own sheeps' wool.

There have been disasters and earth-shaking events as well. I will never forget waking to an early morning earthquake and sitting up to see the apple trees outside the bedroom window lashing back and forth in a wild dance. It seemed these normally sedate trees were enjoying their bacchanal, and we were lucky, suffering no damage. Since we moved here, there have been windstorms and rainstorms, power outages and ice storms. We have learned to keep fuel and a single-burner propane stove, a five-gallon bottle of water, and a store of candles and flashlights for winter emergencies. Though we added a furnace and heat ducts to the house a few years ago, we still supplement our heat with a wood stove, a necessity in power outages, and Bill is usually about two years ahead on firewood stacked in the shed he built out back from wood salvaged when the old barn collapsed one stormy January day.

So, I do not mind being attendant to the repasts of livestock. I believe that the apple trees enjoy their occasional dancing. I once even caught myself talking to a daphne bush: "You're looking well today!" And remembered the transforming myth. Going round to visit each day's new bloom of daylilies on summer mornings seems to me a holy meditation, a kind of prayer wheel.

The faces of the sheep peering out of their winter fleece, the zest of the dogs with their greedy all-sniffing noses, the fierce grace of the cats, the odd dinosaur-like perambulations of the hens with their beady, shuttering eyes and leathery yellow feet. Water, wine, life and death, love and birth. It all sounds familiar.

Once more I imagine the animal world through the eyes of my baby grandson. I am entering the dim barn. There is a smell of straw and manure, dust and sweet alfalfa. Something is coming. The monster thrusts its face close to yours and lets out a roar. You scream once. Then you learn you can live with it. You may even love the creature.

Acknowledgments

⟨⟩

My thanks to Linfield College for giving me sabbatical time and support to finish *Peace at Heart*; to Margaret Scarborough for reading the essays at an early stage and giving advice and encouragement; to Kareen Sturgeon, whose botanical knowledge and field work are a constant source of inspiration and enlightenment; to Molly Gloss and Ursula Le Guin for their very helpful suggestions in revision; to Lex Runciman for being a sounding board for a variety of doubts and questions; to Rick Cooper for copy editing; and to the staff at OSU Press, Warren Slesinger, Tom Booth, and Jo Alexander, for their help and support in bringing this book to print.

"Hiving the Swarm" and "Lamb" originally were published in *Northwest Magazine* (The Oregonian Publishing Co.). "Scalpina" originally was published in *Northwest Magazine* under the title "Henpecked." "Drit" originally appeared in a different, shorter version as "Territory" in *Cold Drill* (Boise State University Press). "Eating Meat" originally appeared in *Rotund World* (Mississippi Mud Productions). "The Gopher and The Gopher Snake"; "Deer Creek, Wet Prairie"; and "Water" first appeared in *Wamka* (Cheahmill Watershed Society), fall 1997, winter 1997, and spring 1998, respectively. "Wild Apples" will appear in *American Nature Writing 1999* selected by John Murray (Oregon State University Press, 1999).

Peace at Heart

Lamb

We'd gotten the sheep the year before, from an ad that read: "spinner's flock reduction." One of the ewe lambs, Amity, seemed undersized, perhaps a drawback in spite of her fine, dense wool. She was slow to mature and when the other two ewes lambed at the end of the next winter, thereby "proving" (as they say in the livestock ads, "proven," like yeast that will rise) the virility of our young ram, Amity showed no sign of maternity. If Ajax, a sturdy black Romney, had managed to breed the other two ewes but not Amity, perhaps our runty ewe was not going to produce. Production, sheep people kept telling us, was everything.

In June, however, when the early lambs already were outsizing their mothers, it became obvious that Amity was going to lamb. Overnight, her udder was as long as her legs and she walked with a dwarfish sway that was brave as it was awkward. With an out-of-season lamb it's hard to tell when to expect it, but one afternoon Amity took off for the barn early so we kept an eye on her.

I have never raised sheep before. Whenever I get a chance I ask a sheep person for details. I do have a copy of Paula Simmons' *Raising Sheep the Modern Way*. I've read it forward and backward and studied the relevant parts as needed, from parasites to subcutaneous injections, from breed types to tips on shearing. The day that Amity went to the barn early I reviewed the section on lambing. With the

1

other sheep, nothing out of the ordinary had happened during lambing except that one night at the end of winter I dreamed about sheep lambing. I got up, as if still in a dream, went out to the barn in red rubber boots and nightgown, and looked into the sheep pen. There was the older ewe, Why, licking off a wet black lamb while the other sheep looked on.

Aurora, the yearling, did more groaning and pacing, but she delivered without assistance. Now I kept an eye on Amity, put her in a pen apart from the others, and hoped she too would deliver well.

About 9 p.m. I went out and checked and found the lamb's nose protruding but no front feet in sight. I went back to the house, where the light was better, and studied the drawings of "abnormal positions in lambing." A lamb is supposed to slide out with its head and front feet pointing downward. According to Paula Simmons, headfirst, feet back is abnormal and needs assistance. A while later I checked for signs of hooves tucked under the lamb's head, which now was dangling under the ewe's tail like some strangely mounted trophy. No feet. For people raised on farms and around animals, such sights may be commonplace. But I am a writer and a college teacher. In middle age and after raising a house full of kids, I am trying to learn how to raise sheep and it's all new to me. *Raising Sheep the Modern Way* describes various obstetrical maneuvers for rearranging a lamb that goes off course in the birth process, most of which involve looping a cord around whatever part of the lamb it is that manages to get itself presented, so as not to lose that part, then gently pushing and turning and reaching in to straighten bent knees and so on. There are various cautions and commentaries regarding not pinching the umbilical cord, which supplies the lamb with oxygen till it's in a position to breathe on its own, and the occasional necessity for delivering a dead lamb, as well as cautions about sanitation and infection. Horrible possibilities presented themselves to my imagination.

I went back to the barn, hoping that Amity would have managed things on her own by now. Perhaps such a short-legged ewe was giving birth to an even shorter-legged lamb, and I was not able to see the feet because they were too short to have appeared yet, but such a possibility did not seem likely. I scanned Paula Simmons' index but there was no entry for "short sheep." The dangling face of the unborn lamb looked both comical and touching. Baby lambs look as if they are smiling, and this head continued to smile with its eyes shut in the sleep of the unborn and its face waxy and wet and unreal, turned downward, absolutely still as if lifeless—and no feet in sight.

To make things worse, Amity seemed to be giving up. She stood up and moved restlessly, bumping the lamb's head against the wall of the barn. She turned dangerously, groaned, and lay down. After a while she seemed to have quit laboring. I bent to look again at the little animal face, unsure in my inexperience if the lamb were, in fact, still alive. It was not breathing, but that would be normal if it were still getting oxygen through its umbilical attachment. I put the flashlight near the lamb's face and its closed eyes twitched in reflex. It was alive. I saw that the lamb's ears were wetly crumpled to its head, and as I reached out and barely touched one it unfolded like a paper flower in water. Amity lay back, her dreamy sheep's eyes resigned. I went to the house for one last look at *Raising Sheep the Modern Way*. I tied three loops of cord as Paula Simmons described. I checked my fingernails for snags and rough spots, and scrubbed my hands and arms with iodine wash, trying self-consciously not to look like a soap-opera surgeon.

Looking for a lubricant, as described, I found nothing that fit the definition of "antiseptic," so I grabbed a bottle of aloe and vitamin E lotion and went to the barn. Considerable time had passed, more than the hour and a half advised by Paula Simmons. Still the birth seemed at an impasse. My husband, who is steadier than I in giving animals shots and holding sheep for shearing, decided his hands were too large to try what we were going to do. I slipped the loop of cord around the back of the lamb's neck and through its mouth as recommended (so as not to choke the lamb). Then I slathered my hands with lotion and slid my right hand along the lamb's neck, into the birth canal. The ewe groaned, as well she might, but she remained still as my husband held her head and the flashlight. For the moment, however, light did not matter. I was thinking of what my fingers saw, and I was reminded oddly of the experience of loading a film developing tank in a light-proof changing bag. As your hands pry apart the film canister and begin to load the film onto the reel, you get the sensation of seeing with your fingertips, while your eyes stare unseeing into the space in front of you.

I moved my hand along the lamb's body, trying to be as gentle as possible, until I felt its shoulder. At one point I thought I felt the umbilical cord looped over the lamb's shoulder and I shrank from entangling it. My hand moved over the lamb's shoulder and down, but at first I could not get a sense of its leg; then I felt the joint of its knee and slid my pointer finger into the bend, pulling the foot forward from where it was turned, slipping it back down the birth canal where it straightened along the lamb's neck and came out.

"The book says it can be delivered with just one leg out," my husband reminded me. I slipped a loop over the protruding foot and gently tugged on this cord and the one that passed across the lamb's neck and through its mouth. The lamb slid out easily now, a limp, small, slippery thing, almost fish-like, but hot and loose, like a soapy washrag. I could not tell whether it was alive. I eased it to the hay-covered floor of the stall and wiped its nose, then it gurgled and gasped, shuddered, and began to breathe.

The ewe looked surprised; this was her first, after all. Then she began to lick the lamb, as it came alive in the straw. The night was warm, so we weren't too worried about cold. The lamb was bony and light, as lambs are, though it would fill out considerably in the next twenty-four hours, and it appeared to be a good-sized lamb. Soon it stumbled to its feet and, swaying amazingly on its tiny hooves, began to look for the ewe's nipple, which I had "stripped"— pulled in a milking motion to clear it of wax. With what looked to me like an agonizing amount of fumbling, ewe and lamb finally got together and she continued to lick it and sniff its rear end, which is the way ewes identify their own lambs, while it nursed in an awkward, off-and-on way.

A newborn lamb makes a tiny *baa* at first, reminiscent of the cry of a human baby; the ewe answers with a soft nicker unlike any of the other voicings sheep make—a sound that attracts, comforts, and quiets the newborn. My husband gave Amity a shot of penicillin to prevent infection from the assisted birth. Then, as soon as it became clear she was doing everything right, we left her with her lamb—a ewe lamb—and went in to bed.

Still awake around 3 a.m., Bill and I went out to the barn to take another look. The lamb was dry now and turned its head to the beam of the flashlight. The ewe nickered and moved defensively to place herself between us and the lamb. My role as obstetrical savior was not about to be appreciated by a sheep. Who ever knows how anything will turn out? But for that moment, it was all right. We went back to the house and slept.

Scalpina

Scalpina was not an ordinary chicken.

No, I cannot say that. Because actually Scalpina was so ordinary I could not distinguish her from her nine sisters. They were already in residence when we moved in. Five of the hens were dark red and five were light red. The people who had owned the farm before us, without a word of warning or advice in their hasty retreat to the suburbs, simply left the chickens. The high grass in the field behind the henhouse was full of spoiled, cracked eggs someone had tossed there. Obviously the people hadn't even been using the eggs. All signs pointed to their having been "soured on the country." The wife had as much as told me so when we first looked at the place. Sometimes people get like that.

But we were pleased to have the chickens. It was a welcome novelty to have fresh eggs and the hens looked strong and healthy, their feathers gleaming with rich color. We grew accustomed to the intonations of their squawks, whether they were complaining about a shortage of drinking water or chicken crumbles, celebrating an egg, warning off jays, or warring among themselves about the occupation of one of the box nests in the henhouse. We cleaned up the henhouse, put in fresh straw, and began to collect beautiful brown eggs for ourselves, for relatives, and for any free-range egg-lover who might come by.

One afternoon when I responded to a bigger fuss than usual, I found a dismal sight. One of the dark red hens lay on the ground, her head pecked to a raw crown of blood. She was alive but battered into a daze. I shooed away the other hens circling around her looking for an opportunity to deliver the *coup de grâce*. There was no doubt about the source of the wounded hen's injuries. I know that hens will sometimes peck an injured hen to death. Whatever had started the peck-in, the hens were anxious to finish it. But I gathered the victim up in a towel and carried her to the house to see what, if anything, I could do.

Bill looked at her and said, "She's a goner." When Bill is confronted with an animal ailment, whether it's fleabite on a dog or diarrhea in a sheep, he is inclined to say: "It's a goner." He is normally a cheerful, optimistic man, so I attribute this reaction to some fatalistic, northern European, generally recessive streak on the Swedish side and let it go at that.

"Well, I don't know," I said. "Maybe not." I salved the hen's scalp with an antibiotic ointment, then took her to the other side of the house, away from the chicken coop. Our house is on a long ridge. To the west, facing the Oregon Coast Range, there is a downslope of sheep pasture, apple trees, the barn, the henhouse, and two or three acres of oak trees. On the east side, there are a small vineyard, a few fruit trees, some bee hives, and several acres of what I can only describe as "habitat." On the crest of this slope in a sheltered spot behind an old shed I placed the red hen, who seemed to be in shock, not obviously suffering, but staring into space with a haunted fixity. Can a hen be "haunted"? I do not believe she was, at that moment, reliving or even remembering the horrors of having the other nine turn on her, like faithless Valkyries. I do not credit hens with much complexity, but one does not have to associate with hens for very long before one realizes the extent of a hen's capacity for arrogance, presumption, and self-satisfaction. I would say that one of the hen's most distinctive traits would be a grandiose sense of self-appreciation. They are strutting, small-minded creatures, obsessed with laying eggs, hiding nests, bickering over tidbits, and preening themselves. When something does not go right, a hen will let you know about it. They are conservatives in all things, and a slight rearrangement of the watering bucket or feed pan, or the arrival of new straw, will send them into a cackle of examination, murmuring, and inspection. In short, they can be interesting characters comparable to some people I know. They are beautiful as well (except when they molt, and then they look like the most miserable, comical figures on earth—Dickensian beggars in tatters of old finery), with dense, red-patterned feathers that catch blue and gold lights from the sun on a summer day.

But our poor scalped hen had lost her luster, not to mention the top of her head. As I dabbed on the antibiotic with a puff of cotton, I realized her assailants had laid back the flesh to the very bone of her tiny skull. I did not want to be cruel to the injured hen by prolonging her life out of anthropomorphic or sentimental impulse, but as she seemed in a shocked but not moribund state I wanted to give her a chance at survival. I arranged a box full of straw, a pan of feed, and some water nearby, and left her to her fate.

The next morning, her fixed stare was gone and she occasionally blinked and cocked her head at the grain pan, though she remained where she was. In the afternoon, however, she had begun to eat and take water, and in a few days her scalp was healing and she began to stroll about the yard. Nevertheless, the part of her head that had been pecked remained hardpan—no skin, no feathers, just a mud-colored sort of scar tissue that made a leathery spot on the top of her head, while the feathers around it grew back in a peculiar crown-like fashion. She was no longer a beautiful chicken, though she would have been identifiable in a crowd.

We had recently gotten a pair of grey China geese, which were about four months old at this time, so I began to feed the hen and the geese together, and the hen took up settling down at night in the proximity of the two geese. The geese were so bonded to one another and so engrossed in their own pursuits that they did not seem very interested in the hen's company, but the three of them stayed more or less together, and when the geese led the hen to their wading pond—a bright yellow plastic basin about five feet across—the hen pressed against the rim of the pool and stared into the water as if to fathom her new companions' interest. Or was she perhaps studying her changed appearance reflected in the water? It reminded me of some lines by Auden, the poet: "Stare, stare in the basin/ And wonder what you've missed." When she in turn led the geese to the area beneath the bird feeder, where she was thrilled to find scattered millet, sunflower seeds, and so on, they looked far less interested than in grass and slugs. But still, though each species failed somewhat in its attempt to show the other a good time, the three fowl kept company day and night, and wandered the field above the vineyard, under the walnut trees.

One day Bill and I were sitting in the yard at the picnic table, cracking walnuts and listening to opera music on a cassette tape player. A powerful piece came on, a song from Verdi's *La forza del destino*. As the singer's voice soared, the hen, whom we could see in the distance, suddenly turned and began a deliberate strut and step toward the music. She crossed the yard, came round the corner of the house, and walked directly to the tape player's speaker, where she stood with her head cocked, staring into the machine from a distance of about twelve inches, until the piece was finished. She then turned and retraced her path to where the geese were slopping around in their pond and stood in humble attendance to their bath.

La forza del destino. Can it be she recognized something passionate in the music? We named her then, Scalpina—the bald-headed Italian opera chicken.

Scalpina lived on the east side of the farm for several months. The geese became full-fledged adults and outgrew her, but still she kept their company, this diminutive red hen with a bald head and a beady eye cocked for worms and crumbles, following slightly behind the geese on their perambulations, a humble attendant to their passions and self-engrossed posturing.

One day in the late fall as I was reading on the porch, I saw the geese parading down the lawn together but Scalpina was not with them. I went around the house but she was nowhere in sight, so I went out to the chicken pen. There she lay at the door of the henhouse, her chicken eyes closed in death, her red feathers dusty. I wondered if nostalgia could operate for a chicken, or if a terminal brain hemorrhage, in preparation since the peck-in of months before, had confused her about where home was. The other hens were milling around but they gave her a wide berth and not one rushed in to peck at her shiny bald head.

Hiving the Swarm

Books on honeybees tell you about "hiving a swarm." All you have to do is go out with a white sheet and any sort of box, preferably "a large hive body with frames and foundation," but lacking that, even a cardboard box will do, temporarily.

Seeing a swarm of bees massed on a tree branch, the books explain, you throw down the sheet under the swarm, put the box on the sheet, then shake the branch or give the swarm a light smack. The mass of bees will drop to the ground in front of the box and run inside. The white sheet makes it easier for you to observe this event, which resembles the opening of the Boston Marathon. I know it actually works like this because my sister told me a neighbor of hers did it this way. I imagine a mass of fuzzy yellow and black bodies in movement toward one goal, the box. One book even says you will thus get to see "your" queen leading the way.

Then you will have a new bee colony.

When Bill told me there was a swarm hanging on one of our plum trees, I decided to try my luck. Fortunately I had just prepared new foundation in some old hive bodies I'd gotten in the fall, for extras. We'd had good luck with the first hive, dividing it, adding extra boxes, or supers, collecting honey. Our fruit crop had never been so abundant and we attributed this to our busy pollinators. Beekeeping seemed almost too easy. I'd gotten the extra supers because I'd been planning to add layers to the two established hives. I surmised this swarm had come from one of them, though when I looked into them none appeared depleted. They were "boiling" with bees, as was proper in the spring. So the swarm might have been wild or from some neighbor's colonies. As a novice beekeeper, I did not know how far a swarm might travel in search of a new home.

I put on my white coveralls, a white plastic helmet with netting and a zipper to attach the netting to the shoulders of my coveralls, and my elbow-length leather and cotton gloves. I tucked the legs of my beekeeping outfit into my boots and went out to the orchard with the empty hive body, a smoker as a precaution (though the books say swarming bees are apt to be docile), and a long pole to knock them out of the tree.

I spread the sheet. I put the hive body in place. With my long pole I knocked the swarm from its branch.

A swarm of bees looks solid. This one was about the size of a large watermelon, and it was compact and stable looking, though its surface moved constantly like the gaseous atmosphere of some strange planet. When I used my pole to separate the swarm from the plum branch, I felt as if I were touching soap bubbles. The swarm dropped to the ground as softly as a ball of fire, like a burning cloud, as if it had no more weight than that. I waited to see *my* queen race to enter the hive, her subjects fast behind her.

Instead, the bees milled around on the ground and shortly began to fly back up to the branch. A couple of bees seemed to inspect the hive body, but their rejection was almost palpable. They returned to the plum branch. An hour later all of the bees were back in a ball hanging from the tree.

I went to another book. It said to wet the bees before trying to "hive" them. "Don't be afraid of drowning any bees," was the direction. All right. I went out with a hose and sprinkled the ball of bees.

Again they fell with a soft plop. A living furball, a black and yellow buzz that spilled and flattened on the sheet. In spite of the book's reassurance, I was afraid I had drowned some bees. I watched them for a while. They just milled around fanning their wings. Of course. What would you do if you had just been doused with a hose? They were drying off. When they were dry, I thought, perhaps they would enter the hive.

An hour later I came out to see that the bees (looking quite dry) had collected on a two foot sucker growing up along the trunk of the plum tree. They made a little mound on the grass and then piled upward on the sucker until there were just a few at the top like determined flagpole sitters. None had entered the hive, but since they were now mostly on the ground in a compact bunch I realized I could "hive" them just by putting the whole box on top of them. This I did. I then stuffed grass in the opening, per directions. "By the time they have chewed the grass away from the opening they will be at home in the hive. Be careful not to block the opening completely or they will suffocate." Of course.

The rest of that day and into the evening I continued to check the hive and was pleased to hear the hum from within. Each time I checked I would see half a dozen bees crawling through the grass and coming and going. I was confident that *my* bees were home to stay.

The next morning they were still in the box. I stood around a bit and finally pulled out some of the grass, feeling they'd earned the assistance. "You will probably have to add another super within 48 hours," the book said, "as they will have already filled the first with comb and brood."

Good.

I checked the hive several times during the day. About three o'clock I went out for another check. The air seemed ominously silent. No bees were coming or going. I stood there in the hot June afternoon, smelling the cherries that were ripening on the nearby trees, the grass that was turning gold and going to seed.

I bent down and pulled off the cover. There was not a bee in sight. In its frame, my new wax foundation, the honeycomb-patterned base that encourages bees to make regular combs, looked possibly a little scuffed, as if shoppers had passed through but left for other markets.

I felt like the child who is left on the wrong side of the mountain in *The Pied Piper of Hamelin*. I tipped my head in the air and listened for sounds of a swarm. Nothing but the house wren burring and fluting on the top of the redwood by the chickenhouse, the geese squawking directions to their eight goslings up by the well, a belch from the ram in the pasture, the commonplace hum of my faithful (for now) older hives going about their business, the distant noises of a hay baler working the slopes down the valley. As if by some enchantment my ear moved out into the sky, listening, listening for a swarm, down the road, into the foothills of the Coast Range, up into the woods where we saw a wild swarm earlier this spring, across the marsh and into a mudbank where we had noticed bees coming and going in a hole in a stump last summer. Listening. Listening. For a mountain to slide apart somewhere and reveal another land all flowers and honey, even better than here.

There is so much I don't know about bees.

Fancy's Lamb

It is Sunday afternoon and Fancy, our brown mother ewe, lies with the other grown sheep in the dusty space under the scrub oaks at the top of the pasture. Her lamb, one week old, dozes a hundred yards away in the grove at the bottom. Fancy looks unconcerned, unmaternal. I need to give the lamb a supplemental bottle feeding of Land-O-Lakes lamb milk replacer, so I walk down the hill and pick him up before he can startle and run away. I carry him back to the house.

Fancy has all but disowned her lamb; we have to hold her head in the barn to let the lamb nurse. As soon as they are back in the field, out of the confined lambing pen, she butts him and scrambles out of reach whenever he tries to eat. Without our feedings he would die.

Born May 29th to a yearling mother, he is late, the last of this season's lambs, but it is not the date of his birth that has turned her from a loving to a neglectful and even abusive mother.

Typically our ewes dote on their lambs. For weeks after they are born, the lambs can hardly get ten feet away without their mothers calling. Ewes panic when new lambs get out of sight. One time we had a five-foot-deep open hole in the yard, a well-meant but soon abandoned attempt to hand-dig a wine cellar in clay soil. A summer storm filled the pit with rainwater. Gamboling lambs are attracted to any little elevation—stumps, hay bales, piles of gravel—where they will prance around, shoving each other this way and that until somebody falls off. Until Bill filled in the pit and smoothed it out, the lambs enjoyed cavorting on the raised circle of dirt at its edge.

I remember one afternoon when Aurora missed her twins and panicked. Baaing frantically, she ran across the field to the edge of the crater. There she stamped her feet, baaed loudly, and craned her neck to stare into the flooded ditch, like any human mother jumping to worst conclusions when the children are late from school. Thus summoned, her lambs, who simply had been adventuring in a nearby blackberry thicket, returned. She nosed them frantically and nickered as they nursed, complacent in the warmth of her attentions.

I have read that this is all induced by natural chemistry. During birth, the pressure of a lamb's head on the cervix and in the vagina causes the ewe's pituitary gland to release oxytocin into the cerebrospinal fluid. This hormonal brain-bath arouses the maternal instinct, expressed in sheep by low-pitched nickering or "baby talk," licking the lamb, sniffing its rear, and sounding high-pitched baaing calls if the lamb is separated from her. Such an explanation does nothing to reduce my amazement at the strength of the maternal instinct. This is normal behavior for a mother sheep: adoration, anxiety, stern remonstration, smug contentment, at least until the lambs begin to outgrow their infancy. Fancy had behaved this way too, for four days, until something happened to disrupt the normal bond.

Fancy had lambed late. Naturally, after our waiting around and staying pretty close to home all during the spring lambing season, when we planned a trip to San Diego and left one of our grown-up children in charge, she chose that weekend to lamb. But everything went well and when we got back from California we found her with a day-old lamb trotting close behind her. She seemed to be doing everything right. She'd given birth in the early morning, cleaned him off without any help, and he was nursing readily without trouble.

He had four days of bliss. Four days of being Fancy's lamby-poo, the center of her universe. Then I made the big mistake.

I had good intentions. In fact, what I did was essential. This well-fed lamb was digesting milk at a great rate and had developed a stinky rear end. That in itself is no problem with lambs, but in this case the debris under his tail had dried to a "plug." When that happens, it's necessary to "unplug." I took him into the laundry room and scrubbed his tail. The accumulation had taken on the character of cement. Unthinking, I squirted hand soap onto his rear and scrubbed until he was relatively clean. I dried him off with a bath towel and returned him to the field where Fancy was frantically running back and forth, baaing and searching for her lost child.

But when I returned him I noticed she wasn't exactly pleased. She sniffed his rear and did a sort of sheep double-take, shaking her head as if to clear her nose of an unpleasant odor. She jerked her head back and looked irritated. He nosed her udder and began to nurse, but she whirled on him and sniffed again, then ran off with the lamb running behind her, as if I had returned the wrong one and she were still searching for *her* lamb. I should have realized something was wrong then, but we had another trip planned (two days this time), we were busy getting organized to leave, and he seemed to be sticking with his mom okay. He knew who *she* was, anyway. He seemed to be getting enough to eat. I gave instructions to Jon, who was watching the place till our return, and we drove out of town.

Two days later, within minutes of our return, I walked through the pasture to see how everyone was doing. I saw Fancy, but no lamb. Startled, I began to search. Jon hadn't said anything about a missing lamb. Most of the sheep were in the top pasture. The lamb wasn't there. I went through the open gate and into the bottom pasture. There I saw the lamb, alone, baaing, and wandering uncertainly in the wrong direction. I picked him up. At once I realized he felt far too light, as if he had been going hungry. I carried him up the hill to Fancy and offered him to her. He was eager for the reunion but when he tried to nurse, she turned and butted him, bowling him over in the long grass. He tried again. She started to butt; he cringed and jumped away, then turned and followed one of the other ewes, futilely trying to grab some nourishment there, then turned to a third ewe who also butted him out of her way. He finally resigned himself to standing alone in the grass, head down, baaing weakly with hunger.

The scene of Fancy shaking her head after I had returned her newly washed lamb suddenly took on meaning. I knew that ewes recognized their lambs by smell, and I had seen it so many times that I should have known it was a mistake to wash the lamb's rear end with soap. If I had used only water it wouldn't have confused the smell. I have since learned that the same hormone that induces other maternal behaviors at birth—oxytocin—is present in "particularly high concentrations in the olfactory bulbs." In other words, from a sheep's point of view, if it smells like my baby, it's my baby. If not, forget it.

It has been two days now since therapy began. We have penned the ewe and lamb together. At first it was particularly rough on him. When he tried to nurse she would knock him down or bump him into the side of the pen. He would stand there uncertainly, staring past her as if to avoid detection. It was hard to watch, but I knew separating them would put an end to any possibility of reconciliation. Forcibly, Bill held her head while I put him on to nurse. We did this several times, and I also squirted him with milk from her udder and rubbed it into his wool. She seemed to be less obstinate about letting him nurse on one side, but when he tried to move to the other side she butted him again. After a day of this she showed no pleasure in the lamb. There were none of the typical greetings, the nickering and baaing that goes on with a properly bonded ewe and lamb.

I was still hopeful of a bonding, however imperfect. An odd experience earlier this year showed me how persistent a lamb can be in the process of survival. Fancy's mother, Why, due to years of nursing vigorous udder-butting lambs, has milk on only one side. She willingly nurses twins and we supplement when needed, but this year I noticed that of her two lambs, a white ewe and a white

ram, the girl always seemed to get the working spigot. The ram—
Lamb Boy—repeatedly seemed to end up on the dry side. I began
to give him a supplemental bottle which he gulped at a great rate.
Supplementing his feed seemed to do nothing to break the bond
between the lamb and Why. He would run to get his feeding when
I called out through the fence, "Here Lamb Boy!" Then he would
return to Why and his sister to wander the pasture or to take a
digestive lie-down in the shade of the oak grove. Why always
welcomed him and performed the usual baaing to call him to come
with her when the flock moved on to a different area.

One day when I offered Lamb Boy a bottle, he seemed less hungry
than before, and I wondered if by some miracle Why had begun
producing milk on the damaged side or if she was just giving so
much milk that she could feed two on one side. Then I noticed
Lamb Boy sidling up to Bela, a large black ewe with a single black
ewe lamb, Gloria, born about the same time as Lamb Boy. Bela is a
mixed breed. The woman who sold her to me called her a
"Coopworth-type." A Coopworth is a registered mixture of Romney
and Lincoln imported from New Zealand, but the Northwest
Colored Wool Growers Association papers that came with her cited
Romney and Shropshire as her antecedents. She has the wool
topknot characteristic of Romneys but she's much taller than the
others, so I'm not sure what she is. When she has a year's growth
on, Bela's long, crimpy fleece stands out around her as if she were
electrified and she is ample in all ways, with big gold eyes and a
heavy, long body on graceful legs. Her udder gushed more than
enough milk for little Gloria. Lamb Boy apparently had noticed. I
saw that he was trying to sneak a swig on Bela. She butted him
roughly away, as sheep mothers do with other ewes' lambs.

Sheep are very strict about this sort of thing. People go to all
sorts of lengths to "graft" a motherless lamb onto a ewe whose own
lamb has died, such as skinning the dead lamb and tying its familiar-
smelling hide over the orphan to fool the grieving mother. And
there are devices used to anchor a sheep so a lamb can nurse without

being pushed away until, it is hoped, the ewe gives up and accepts the alien lamb. But it isn't easy. Obviously there is a strong taboo against udder altruism in the sheep world.

Lamb Boy continued to take his bottle feeding, occasionally trying to get a snack from his true mom while his sister got most of the goodies, and at the same time persisted in trying to nurse from Bela. Because of Bela's long legs, her udder is well up in the air and a little more accessible than on some of our shorter ewes whose full udders nearly drag the ground and are hidden behind their massive, grass-digesting bellies. I noticed that Lamb Boy tended to follow Gloria around, shadow-like, approaching Bela by standing slightly behind and between her and Gloria. When Gloria would begin to nurse, Lamb Boy would duck under Bela's rear end, right between her back legs, and grab a snack from the opposite teat. More and more he was getting away with it. Sometimes he would make the mistake of going to the opposite side from Gloria, the usual position for a nursing twin, right out in plain sight. So arranged, twin lambs will nurse while the mother alternately sniffs their familiar twin rear ends to make sure they are who they should be. When Lamb Boy tried this with Bela, he would get knocked down at first sniff and lose his chance. But if he dived under from the rear she would sniff at Gloria on her left, then look to the right, see nothing, and somehow not notice Lamb Boy sneaking in the back way. By this device he soon adapted to nursing from Bela, to the point that he began to refuse the bottle—an unheard-of adaptation in my experience. When I pointed out what was going on, Bill said, "Oh, no, a smart sheep!" It was true.

Oddly enough, though Bela still butted Lamb Boy away when she caught him snacking, she often didn't catch him, and she seemed gradually to accept his company as she moved about the pasture. And since his true mother, Why, and her ewe lamb also tended to group with Bela and Gloria, this meant that the five sheep—two mothers with three lambs between them—often tended to graze together and then take their ruminating lie-down together.

Moreover, Gloria and her adopted brother and his sister seemed to form a play group—for instance, when it was time to play jump-on-the-stump. It's the first example I've seen of a sheep "alternative family," and even as the lambs approached weaning age it was still working.

However, Fancy seemed not to be so amenable as Bela. Even though we had penned her with her lamb and under restraint she had allowed him to nurse, she still exhibited little maternal response. Of one thing I was sure: the lamb had the will to survive. But my tendency to see human qualities in animals had gone into high gear and I sadly noted small changes in his behavior that suggested abuse. Ewes and their lambs do a lot of voicing. At birth, the mother nickers in a tiny baby-talk voice as she cleans her lamb and nudges it to stand up and eat. When she moves back into the field with the lamb, she frequently baas to signal it to keep up, and the lamb responds with a tiny baa saying "here I am, here I come." If a lamb falls asleep in tall grass and fails to keep up with the continual movement that goes with grazing, the ewe may not worry—until she suddenly realizes her lamb is nowhere to be seen. Then she sets up a loud, urgent baaing until the lamb awakes and replies. In other words, "I call—you answer" is the lesson lambs imbibe along with their mother's milk.

With Fancy's lamb, the vocalizing didn't work. Fancy would occasionally baa to her imagined "other" lost lamb, the one that smelled right. When her lamb approached, baaing, and tried to nurse, she would smell him, shake her head to rid her nose of the unhappy smell, butt him violently, and run off as if she'd just seen a snake. Thus negatively reinforced, the lamb quit baaing. He also adopted a more wary attitude. There is usually nothing so carefree as a lamb. They gambol and chew and nurse and run in a little herd of their peers. They get baaed over and fed by their mothers, indulgently and carefully sniffed and stepped over by the rams. If a dog or an irritable goose appears, mother will step between the intruder and her lamb, providing worry-free passage to the water trough or the upper pasture. But Fancy's lamb had lost these protections. What the other lambs took for granted he had to work to try to snatch—with the reward usually a sip of milk at most and then a butting. He had learned to grab for a snack and then leap out of the way. He looked tense and confused.

After a day of confinement in the lambing pen, however, Fancy seemed, if not actually enjoying his company, at least somewhat more indulgent. Now and then he would get a quick meal. I continued to squirt some of her milk into his wool and rub it in. I even picked him up and rubbed him over some of the grubbier spots on her body, to try to give him more of her smell, and she seemed a little less repulsed by his odor. In her isolation in the barn, Fancy had kept up a steady baaing for the company of the other ewes, out enjoying the long June grass. Worried that minimal nursing and a lack of good green food might cause her milk to dwindle, I decided to try them in the pasture. She looked as if she had decided he wasn't too bad after all. Well, that was a mistake. As soon as I opened the barn gate, she charged off at high speed to join the other ewes, leaving the forlorn black lamb trotting uncertainly through the high grass with no one to turn to. I broke down and brought him a bottle of milk replacer, picked him up and gave him half an hour of petting and scratching, hoping that would in some small measure make up for the neglect. I'd seen films of motherless monkeys; without the comfort of touch they did not flourish. Sheep touch is different from monkey touch and certainly from human touch, but there is a definite system of close contacts, of smells and sniffings and of lying down together to ruminate.

Very young lambs enjoy climbing on their mothers, sometimes even nestling down on their mothers' woolly backs to nap, and during lie-downs they often position themselves out of the wind behind their mothers' broad backs. There are slight variations in herding behavior in different breeds and from one individual to another, but in general, sheep have strong flocking instincts. They need to be with other sheep and they move together as they graze, and lie down together when they ruminate or sleep. This instinct is so strong, I think it must be cruel to isolate a sheep unless there is a donkey or a horse or some other companion to graze with. I've noticed only two occasions for separation in our sheep. One is that the rams hang out together in one part of the field and the ewes hang out together in another, except in breeding season, of course, when the rams follow the ewes and turn competitive with one another. The other is when a ewe is about to lamb—she will sometimes go off by herself into the woods and usually will stay somewhat apart from the other ewes when her lamb is brand new, presumably to protect the lamb and reinforce the bond between them without the confusion of other sheep too near. But neither of these behaviors applied to Fancy and her lamb.

After I fed the lamb, he trailed uncertainly behind the other sheep, several times falling asleep and letting them wander off into an entirely different area without a concerned mother baaing to let him know where he should be. That night we put the pair in the lambing pen again and it was as if there had been no progress at all. He tried to nurse. She butted him, sniffed, snorted, tried to get away. Bill held her head, I put him on to nurse, Fancy resented the whole ordeal, and the lamb stood unhappily with his head down, cowering in a corner lest his mother deliver the descending blow that would knock him up against the wall. It was a miserable commentary on sheep motherhood.

What if we were putting the lamb and Fancy through all this for nothing? What if the broken bond was irrevocable? He had, after all, had four days of blissful nursing at the most important time, getting all the colostrum and early milk that would bestow immunities and get his system going. We could bottle feed him for eight weeks and by that time he could get along on Fatena and grass. There's something appealing about raising a "bummer," a motherless or outcast lamb. We raised Cleo, a weak third in a set of triplets. Cleo would happily hang out with the rest of the sheep, and when she was hungry she would slip through the fence, come to the back door, and baa. We'd open the door and her little hooves would go click-click across the kitchen linoleum. Bill or I would give her her bottle. She'd drink till she was full, then turn and click-click out and through the fence and back with the sheep again. Cleo turned out to be a wonderful adult Romney ewe, mother of robust, happy, well-adjusted lambs—no problems there.

But Cleo's mother hadn't rejected her. Cleo had simply been unable to compete with her two larger brothers in a two-teat world, and rather than let her fall behind we took on the bottle job. I couldn't help feeling that there was something to be gained if we could reestablish the bond between Fancy and her lamb before her milk quit. I decided to give it two whole days of isolation this time, no matter how she hollered.

Every few hours we went through the routine of making sure he was able to nurse without being butted. After a day or so she seemed to be adapting. After two days she actually nickered and smelled his rear as he nursed without trying to clear her nose of his odor. On the third day I asked Bill, "Do you think it will work?" We opened the barn door.

Fancy stood there a moment like a prisoner blinking in the sudden sunlight. Then she bolted into the pasture, leaving little black lamb behind in the dark barn. My heart sank. The unnatural bitch! She didn't care a bit. Thoughts of selling her at auction ran through my head.

Then she stopped short. The other ewes were in the distance, in the deep green grass of the lower pasture. She stared at them. Then she turned her head and baaed behind her. The lamb came out into the sunlight. She nickered and sniffed his rear end. He took a couple of reassuring drafts of mother's best lunch; she sniffed him again and baaed reassuringly. They trotted down the field. He was so close to her side she might have stepped on him, but she didn't. She was very careful and nickered him all the way back to the flock.

Neighbors

Coming home to a driveway full of official-looking cars is never a calming sight. I'd spent the morning at my office in town. Now, my stomach tightened when I saw a woman in uniform standing by the county sheriff's vehicle in front of my house. She was writing in a notebook and looked serious. My husband glanced up from speaking to her and walked toward me as I jumped out of the car.

"Dog attack," he said. I saw that the other unfamiliar vehicle belonged to the vet, just now going to the barn with his bag of instruments.

"Who was it?" I didn't know for sure whether I was asking which of the sheep had been attacked and how badly, or which dog it was, and whose, but I hurried into the barn to see for myself. The vet went down on his knees in the lambing stall where one of our white ewes lay, most of her wool torn off and her stocky sheep's body a mass of blood and wounds. I could hardly recognize her, but it was Bonnie George, the ewe whose late birth a year and a half before had been my first (and so far, only) experience with a problem delivery. Saving her and her mother had been a satisfying victory in my early adventures with animal husbandry. This spring, she was due to deliver her own first lamb, but from the gashes and bite marks all over her body I doubted that would turn out well.

Bill explained that he had seen a neighbor's dog, a large, black, mixed breed, come running out of our barn when he and our daughter Robin came up the driveway from a walk. The dog ran off down the road. In the barn, Bill found one sheep with bite marks. He counted heads, found a number of the flock huddled in various parts of the field, scattered and frightened, then realized that Bonnie George was missing. Following a messy trail of blood and bloody wool, he found her deep in a blackberry thicket. To reach her, he used a machete to hack away at the brambles that had been her refuge and apparently had stopped the dog from finally killing her. Then, with the barnyard wheelbarrow, Bill carted her to the lambing stall where she now lay. His own clothes were covered with blood from wrestling her torn, heavy body into the wheelbarrow. Once all the sheep were accounted for, Bill called the vet and the animal control officer.

The dog that had attacked the sheep had been running loose for several months, and we had called the owners more than once when we'd seen him running down our driveway or crossing the pasture. One morning I found that something had gotten two of the gray geese—one was dead in the walnut grove with bite marks in its back, and the other was missing. A trail of bloody feathers led to the road. I called the dog's owner and asked whether the dog had brought home a dead goose.

"Why, he wouldn't hurt a thing. He's just a pup. We wouldn't want him to hurt anybody. We like your geese, they're real pretty."

"I wish you wouldn't let him run like that. We've got livestock here."

"We'll look around and see if he got a goose, but I sure don't think so. I wouldn't keep a dog chases livestock."

"You can't let a dog run," I said.

"It's mean to tie a dog up in the country. He won't hurt nothing."

I didn't relish getting into a fight with the neighbors, so I hoped they'd act on my calls. But several times in the early morning we saw the dog crossing the field below our place, and a couple of times we saw him—a galumphing, big, puppy-like dog, less than a year old but already weighing seventy pounds or more—chasing his owners' car down the road as they drove to town.

"I should have called the police the first time that dog came on our place," I muttered. "I shouldn't have given him the chance."

So much for hindsight. I thought about how people talk about coyotes attacking sheep, but from talking with other sheep people and from reading I've learned that most predator attacks on sheep are by domestic dogs. City people who move to the country often idealize the freedom of the place and naively project their feelings onto their dogs. The idea that in the country you can let your dog run loose is one of the most prevalent delusions among newcomers to country life. Even when people are pressured into restraining a dog during daylight hours, irresponsible owners often let their dogs out at night to "get some exercise."

On the other hand, old-timers say that in the country you can shoot any dog that trespasses on your property. Do it, they say, and predatory dogs won't become a problem. But what if shooting dogs is not something you feel comfortable doing? Or even if it is, in the country these days homes are close enough, people abundant enough, that someone shooting at a dog crossing the yard just might hit a neighbor—or at least a neighbor's window. As one who has had a sunroom window shot out by thirty-year-old neighbor "boys" having fun with a long-range rifle ("We never knew there was a house back there"), and who has seen the bullet hole in another neighbor's deck after passing hunters fired at an elk crossing her pasture, I am not casual about shooting, even in the country.

Besides, I like dogs. The dog that attacked our sheep, and probably our geese, was acting on his own natural instincts. He was not a bad dog, just a neglected one. It was the owners who had been at fault. I felt sorry for the dog, but once he had attacked our sheep, bitten two, and ripped the body of one with literally hundreds of deep bites that left the flesh hanging from her throat and side like bloody rags, there was no alternative. According to law, the dog had to be destroyed and the owners had to pay fines and reparation for damage to our animals.

"It was him. No two ways about it," said the animal control officer. "All the way in the truck he kept vomiting wool and blood after we picked him up. He about choked on it. He was full of it."

In the meantime, we had one badly injured sheep to deal with as well as two others with lesser but real injuries. And we expected that all of our ewes were pregnant, so there was the possibility of losing some of the lambs, due to the dog chasing the flock up and down the pasture. Since they were early on in their pregnancies, we could only guess, if a ewe failed to produce a lamb in March, that she might have miscarried due to the dog attack.

That was a future worry. For now, the vet explained that Bonnie George's wounds were too ragged and too deep to stitch—there would be problems with drainage in the infected wounds and there was simply no effective way to stitch her ripped flesh back together. Instead he cleaned her off—there was little wool left on her back—cleaned the wounds, used tape where necessary, put an ointment all over her raw skin, and pressed a loose gauze over the worst spots. He gave her antibiotics and left us with medication and instructions. He told us to freshen the dressing and ointment every day, give her a full course of antibiotics, and keep her warm.

Since it was January, the air was still chilly, especially in the dim shelter of the barn. Although she was covered with bites, Bonnie George had not bled to death and the vet said that she could recover as long as we worked to prevent infection—and, most difficult of all, as long as she could be persuaded to eat. Animals traumatized by such injuries often refuse to eat and they eventually die.

We bought a heat lamp to hang over the lambing pen, to keep her torn and woolless body warm. I tore up an old nightgown and used the flannel to line a grey wool army blanket, which I sewed into a kind of shawl to cover her back. Bonnie George was in a stupor of misery as she sat in the stall, under the reddish glow of the heat lamp, in her grey woolen blanket-cape, staring through the curious horizontal eye slits of her kind, into some unimaginable sheep oblivion. She did not try to get up, or to stretch out, but merely huddled motionless. And in fact, she would neither eat nor drink. I was determined she would survive, so I began using a gravy baster to dribble water into her mouth, along with doses of glycol now and then, to give her energy. When she would not go for the molasses-flavored corn-oats-barley mixture (COB), I took small amounts of the sweet-smelling COB and stuck it in her mouth. Gradually, instead of letting the grain fall to the straw-covered floor of the pen, she began to chew. I did this several times a day, waiting for her to show some sign of her former, alert personality.

Bonnie George was a name my husband had given her. She was born during our first year of lambing, the "B" year. We had given "A" names to the sheep we bought for our starter flock, then "B," and so on. The "D" year was coming up. I don't know why he called her Bonnie George but it had an odd, humorous quality that seemed to fit. She was an inquisitive Romney ewe with a nice, crimpy, cream-colored fleece. Her forelock, a patch of wool growing low on her forehead, characteristic of Romneys, was thick and curly and stood up in a perky, surprising way. Along with the dense ruff around her neck, like the collar of some Dutch burgher out of a Rembrandt painting, this bristling forelock gave her an attentive, continually amazed expression. Now all of this soft expressive wool had been ripped and torn away and she was a pathetic sight. With her exposed pink skin and the flannel cape I tucked over her back, she looked like someone's ailing grandmother.

One day, after about a week of stunned immobility under the heat lamp, regular force feedings, daily coating with medicated ointment, and cleaning and readjustments of her blanket and straw, Bonnie George stood up and turned around in the pen. She was going to live.

Though she was badly scarred, during the next year her wool grew back, covering the pale jagged tissue. Still on her neck are pockets where the skin was torn away from the flesh and failed to reattach, but when we sheared the sheep this year Bill carefully trimmed around the damage. It gives her a peculiar look, but she seems healthy and as calm as any of the sheep. She even produced a lamb. I wondered about the effect of the dog attack, of her not eating, and of the medications, but the lamb seemed in good shape. She liked the lamb a lot, as sheep mothers do, and though we didn't need an extra ram, out of deference to her ordeal and against the principles of the market, we kept him and named him Dirty Hairy. Not that he is less hygienic than any other sheep—he's very nice, in fact. He's short but stocky and has a marked and useful propensity for eating blackberries, poison oak, and hawthorn shoots—a definite brush sheep, something to appreciate on an overgrown old farm like ours. At night when the sheep come into the barn, if there is one missing it's apt to be Dirty Hairy, who is somewhat of a loner and inclined to be off in the deep of the woods eating something stickery. This makes me wonder about prenatal influences on sheep. His name, suggesting Clint Eastwood's film persona and far from an insult, is a tribute to his toughness in being born at all, given the odds, and is descriptive of the odd grey-brown spots on his hide and his abundant curly wool. So Bonnie George did not lose her lamb, though another expensive brown sheep we had recently bought to add variety to the flock did. And a year later, Bonnie George produced a bonus in black-and-white twins, one of them a white ram and one of them a peculiarly attractive brown ewe with dense dark ringlets of wool and an alert tilt to her ears and head.

I still have to remind myself that if I see another dog running loose through our place I will need to do something about it right away and not wait for half-hearted warnings to be acted on. We have two dogs ourselves, and I know that they would have a great time chasing sheep were they allowed to run wild. From a dog's point of view, dogs chase, sheep run; what could be more amusing?

Talking to the neighbors who owned the dog was painful. The husband accepted responsibility, no argument about it. He apologized in a forthright way, and saw to it that reparation was made. The wife, I am sorry to say, responded differently. The animal control officer warned us that she was definitely going to be unfriendly: "She pouted and cried and said, 'What do they have to keep sheep here for anyway?' She says she's going to get another dog so you might watch out. She's one of those bleeding heart types, thinks it's cruel not to let a dog run loose." I thought of the expensive flock of cashmere goats at the other end of the road and the various other flocks of sheep in the neighborhood. I wondered at the woman's lack of consideration.

This is a small community. In the grocery story a while after that I found myself standing in line ahead of the husband. It was awkward. "Hello," I said.

"Hello," he said. "Real sorry about your sheep."

"Yes," I said. "Well, thanks for taking care of things."

"It's all right," he said.

Outside the store, the wife was in the car. When I came out of the market she pointedly turned her head away, tilting her nose up in a classic demonstration of the cold shoulder.

And so she continues to do, if she is in the yard as we pass on the road, walking our dogs. She who had come to our door trying to sell Avon products and who had dropped in when we first came to the neighborhood to gossip about water rights and gardens and who else lived nearby.

"Maybe if you'd bought some of her Avon stuff," my husband suggests, only half joking.

Even in the country, it's not always easy to stay on good terms with the neighbors.

Wild Apples

Below our vineyard is a brushy area which when we first moved to the farm I tended to think of as a narrow border or hedge, a small place. It was difficult to get in to look around because some former owner had bulldozed an old prune orchard off the hill and pushed the dirt and brush into a rough line across the property. This line of dirt and stumps had grown up in blackberries, wild rose, and hawthorn, presenting a thorny thicket that defied entry until Bill took the tractor and a machete and alternately mowed and hacked a gateway into the brush. Stepping through the hedge for the first time, I had the elevated, free feeling I get from my recurrent dream about finding a secret room in an old house, the realm of newly discovered possibilities.

Beyond the thicket the brushy area turned out to be large, about four or five acres, not merely a hedgerow at all, and while some parts were impenetrable, much of it consisted of a maze of tiny meadows defined by a variety of trees and bushes. Much of the larger growth turned out to be apple trees. It was spring when I first stepped through to the secret side of the hedge and found myself meandering down alleys of flowering trees, fragrant and electrically alive with the sound of bees.

Spring went by and the apple blossoms turned to little green knobs, then apples. Summer went by and the apples took on various shapes and colors. In late September, I decided to spend a day tasting apples. At first I had thought the apple trees were the remains of an overgrown domestic orchard, but then I realized they were wild seedlings in an amazing variety. Apple trees for domestic and commercial use are produced by grafting the desirable scion onto a suitable root stock, to get predictable results. Thus the fruiting branches are clones of the mother tree.

On the other hand, apples grown from seed, like those in our wild patch, are highly unpredictable. You don't know which ancestors they will resemble. They may be attractive and good tasting, but they also may be runty, warty, hard little objects that pucker the mouth like a dose of alum, dry out the tongue with astringency, and leave a lingering bitterness. The variety in the hidden grove made it clear that these were apples that had been left to their own devices.

Tasting wild apples one begins to realize how many factors play a part in the enjoyment of a good apple. I thought of what I might find. Color: red, yellow, or green; blushing, solid, or streaked. Heft: the weight in the hand that signals the density and juiciness of the apple meat. Character of skin: russet or smooth, tough or fine, waxy or squeaky clean. Taste: sour or sweet or bitter, resonant in the mouth or flat and insipid. Fragrance, suggestive of honey or lemons, strawberries or bananas, willow bark or grape seeds. The way the apple releases or does not release its juice when you bite it. Whether it is pulpy or mushy, or cracks with a satisfying crunch. And beyond the immediate sensation of eating the apple itself are qualities such as whether it's a keeper or not, the time of ripening, whether it bruises easily, and how well it resists pests and disease. Clearly I was in for an adventure.

I took a pack with colored pens and pencils, a small notebook, my camera bag, tripod, and coffee, hollered for the dogs, and set off for my secret orchard. To begin this wild apple adventure, I decided to use my camera. The process of photographing can sharpen observation. As I became engrossed in the process of framing images, changing lenses to move up on the fruit, changing again to get the wide shape and pattern of a tree studded with red or yellow pomes, I began to see how really different the many apples were. Some were pure yellow and small, only a couple of inches across. These tended to be abundant on the tree and bitter tasting. They are the kind you see in hedges in midwinter, still hanging, like ornaments, on a leafless tree. Some were longer and narrower; others were squat and fat, almost wider than they were long from stem to blossom end. Some were green with a purplish cheek and others were heavily russeted. One pretty little apple was such a pale green it looked almost white and had bright red cheeks. Had I been naming it, I would have called it Snow White or candy cane. As I looked through my camera at close range, I enjoyed focusing on the ones where the red streaking consisted of distinct stripes, particularly those where the red appeared on a background of deep waxy yellow so that the overall color of the apple seemed dark orange.

Because it was September, the leaves were starting to turn and fall from the trees, and many apples also had fallen. I had seen pheasants going in and out of the thicket and wondered whether they enjoyed the apples. Here and there were the droppings of deer and of squirrels, and I saw a downy woodpecker traveling along one dead branch scattering moss and bark in his excavations. Surely all this fallen fruit could feed a variety of creatures. In spite of all the apples on the ground, the trees still were covered with fruit. I wondered how old the trees actually were. Some of them were good sized but others were small and poorly grown, with only a live branch or two jutting out at a strange angle, holding a clutch of apples. Many of these smaller trees had more dead limbs than live ones, and the whole tree was covered with a heavy growth I supposed was lichen, dry and whitish grey now, but which I knew would gather moisture and flourish in the wet western Oregon winter. Besides the lichen, the trees were draped with brambles and cheek to cheek with hawthorns covered by dark red haws. Great bunches of wild rose briars, with orange and red hips, thrust up and blended with the apple branches, so that the trees looked ancient and hoary and tangled like an illustration from an old book of fairytales.

I used up a couple of rolls of film. The day was hot and I was beginning to feel it as I moved through the protected little meadows, so I decided it was time to begin my taste testing. I picked as wide a variety of apples as I could reach without getting into the poison oak (another element in the tangle of brush), and dropped them—about thirty-five or forty altogether—in a comfortable grassy spot where I could sit in the shade and concentrate. Looking upon the variety they presented, I remembered reading that the ancient Romans described and recognized thirty-seven domestic types of apples. I also had heard that in the original apple forest, in southwest Asia, in the Caucasus region, there were well over 3,000 varieties of wild apple. I wondered to what extent the wild genes in my apples had reconstituted those early assortments.

I told Mollie and Jack, our border collies, to sit down and pay attention, and they threw themselves into a shady thicket and stretched out with panting grins as I continued my apple meditations. A small airplane flew over, dipped low, circled around and came back over my clearing as if to see what I was up to, and then, having taken his glimpse of Eden, the pilot flew on.

I had decided that if I found a wild tree with especially good apples I would tie a rag to one of its branches, to mark it out for future use and observation. There were, after all, at least two hundred wild trees in this little acreage.

One by one I would choose a particular apple, make a quick sketch of it with colored pencil, and then write a description of it in the margins of the drawing. The first apple I chose was a yellow one, not very tasty but not inedible. Its appearance interested me because the lenticels, or pores, on its skin were lighter than the yellow of the skin itself and gave the apple's surface a shimmering, pearlescent appearance that reminded me of boiling sugar. Pretty, but nothing to tie a flag on. The second apple was a wonderful surprise. It was large as wild apples go, the size of a baseball. It was a waxy yellow with a heavy overlay of red striping, like certain varieties of French apples, and had pronounced ribs that gave the whole apple a scalloped appearance. I wondered whether the undulations of its shape were genetic or due to some warping disease. The meat cracked pleasantly when I bit into it and the flesh inside was golden yellow, very juicy, fragrant, and distinctive. I didn't see any worm holes but after I had eaten most of it, I broke the core in two to get a look at the seeds and found that some Epicurean critter dining there had reduced the seeds to a fine dust of black droppings. I decided I would definitely tie a flag on this tree to keep track of it, as it was an apple I would find a treat in any company.

The next apple was green with a purplish blush. It had a particularly hard, smooth look. I held it in my hand and stared at it, trying to be alert to its character, and it seemed like a smooth and placid face—a pacific, contained, nun-like apple. I took a bite. It was not fully ripe but its taste and its dense, firm flesh indicated it would be a good keeper, a late, winter apple compared to my delicious scalloped apple which obviously was at the height of its taste and condition. This keeper, my nun-apple, looked evenly spaced on the tree, uniform in size, regular in form and color, almost like a cultivated apple. I gave it a flag.

I tasted many other apples, but most I was happy to cede to the wildlife. I found that I could not predict from the appearance of an apple how it would taste. One tree bore nice red fruit whose appearance made me expect something like a small Jonathan, but the apples were nasty tasting in the extreme. Another tree had apples that were green and hard looking and markedly ovoid in shape, but the meat was wonderfully sweet, pale yellow, with darker yellow honey spots growing even sweeter near the core and no apparent pests or disease.

I almost skipped the tiny crab apples from one small tree that already had lost almost all its leaves because the apples were so tiny and purplish green, their skin matte-looking and covered by a dusty bloom. The apples hung in groups of four at the ends of long, red, wire-like stems and were about the size of large marbles, but I decided to try them while I was at it and was surprised and delighted that they were crunchy and juicy, with clear yellow flesh and a sweet lemony taste with no hint of bitterness at all. The core was small and contained perfect clean little seeds, almost black in color.

It was late in the afternoon when I picked up my bag of pencils and other gear. The restless dogs took off running toward the house as soon as I stood up. Before I stepped through the hedge and back into the order of the vineyard with its vines and trellises, I looked around, and in every direction, gleaming in the yellow sunlight, I saw the temptation of farther apples, more apples. I wanted to taste them all.

Uphill I saw the neat rows of the vineyard serving our human designs. Downhill was the chaotic beauty of wild groves. What a misbehaving, divided mind I have, approving of tidy gardens and fenced pastures, yet feeling such glee that wild apples have their own ineffable plans, if only we leave them alone.

The Ram

They say a ram is one-half the flock. In production terms, this is certainly true, for the ram contributes his genes to all of the lambs, whereas each ewe imparts her characteristics to her lamb or lambs alone. From his grand position as sire of the flock, you might think a ram would develop a sense of arrogance, as I suppose he does, but he does not show it in the way you might expect.

Sometimes, if there are young ram lambs, teasers (infertile rams), wethers (gelded rams), or particularly other rams around, the chief ram will assert his dominance by lowering his head and charging, over and over, until either he or his challenger has had enough. Enough usually means at least a bloodied head, which is a gory sight and can be dangerous, even fatal, if infection sets in. Most of the time, however, males in a group seem content to hang out together and eat grass. Penned together, they sometimes will do a certain amount of lightweight "boxing." Or they will charge and feint, ducking to one side or the other before they actually crash— though a persistent challenger may get the full, head-bloodying treatment. That they often feint then duck to one side, in a fairly coordinated manner, indicates to me that there is some sort of communication going on, like the eye signals that keep well-adjusted people from walking into one another on the sidewalk.

Still, a butting ram is not something to turn your back on. I was once the target of a ram's charge, and I don't intend to let it happen again, because even charging at a distance of about three feet in a small pen, a ram can do a lot of damage and make you think seriously about hurting him in return—which is unworthy, I believe, of shepherding. The time he butted me, I had come into the barn to find a ewe lambing and began to climb over the fence into the pen. I didn't notice Ajax, our big grey Romney, who immediately charged out of the darkness and hit me on the leg. I socked him futilely in the head with my fist and staggered into the pen, where he turned aside at my yelling and looked as docile as a sausage, showing no more inclination to give me trouble. I didn't trust him, though, and with one hand grabbed him by the chin, forcing his head up and out of butting position, and with the other hand grabbed him by the rump in order to move all 250 pounds of him out of there so I could get a look at the ewe. It wasn't easy.

A ram is thick-headed, literally. All you have to do is feel his forehead, give it a scratch or two, and you will sense the resonance of thick, compacted bone under woolly hide, as if you were patting the head of, say, a carpeted stone lion. The term "battering ram" is not a bad description. However, for all his toughness with the guys, our ram usually is a gentleman when it comes to persuading the ladies.

An effective ram is supposed to have a "good nose" to start with. That means he can tell when one of the females is in heat by sniffing. It's important because the ewe's fertility cycle is short, about seventeen hours. In other words, the ram has to be ready when opportunity knocks. All very well, but there is more to it than that. A ram who suspects that one of the ladies is in the mood will approach from the rear and tap on the ground with one hoof. If the grazing is good or she is not impressed, she may ignore him and he will have to tap again, whereupon she usually will squat slightly, without missing a bite of grass, and urinate. The ram will sniff and turn his nose up into the wind, wrinkle his upper lip, and get a faraway look in his eyes while exposing his teeth in an expression that looks a little like someone very la-di-da tasting wine. If the vintage is right, he will make his move, but there is no strong-arm behavior here. Instead of pushing the ewe around, the ram is apt to sidle up to her flank and nicker, a soft little nicker, very like the babytalk of ewes to their new lambs. I imagine he is saying something to the effect of, "little baby lamby love, ooo big rammy wam is right here by your side" and so on. She may walk away for a patch of grass three feet down the field and he will follow, sniff, tap his hoof, and nicker again, all the while flicking his tongue in and out with a suggestive gesture I haven't seen the likes of since the rock group KISS. On it goes, paw, sniff, nicker, flick the tongue, nudge her flank, nicker, nicker. . . There usually is no rough stuff. If she is attracted, she may "stand for him" immediately. If she is indifferent or merely feeling pestered, she will move on, with the ram close behind, until she decides to pay some attention—which, if he acts cute enough, will not be too long.

All in all, the courtship gestures of the ram are amazingly gentle. Persistent, yes, but also very gentle. Persuasive, and a bit comical from a human viewpoint. Maybe the ram looks a little silly, like an adolescent boy reading the *Sports Illustrated* swimsuit issue, but in fact his gentle attitude toward the ewes pays off. I know there are rams who get their way by being rough, but the gentleness of our ram, Ajax, is impressive, particularly given his innate inclination to get his way simply by throwing his 250 pounds of weight behind that stony skull of his. If he's going to maintain his position as half the flock, he'd better know how to treat the other half right.

Eating Meat

Until we started raising sheep, I had never eaten an animal I'd raised. Wool, not meat, was on my mind when we got the starter flock. To learn more about sheep, my husband and I went to various sheep association events, and learned that a lamb barbecue was invariably part of the deal.

The schedule of events would include, perhaps, a sheep dog demonstration. Then there'd be a "bummer" show, bummers being the orphaned or rejected lambs raised by bottle. Many of the bummers were raised by farm children who would show their sleek, pampered lambs in ribbons or hats, or perhaps in ribbon traces, pulling a play cart and being seduced into the ring by a handful of molasses flavored grain.

Other standard sheep-day events included showing of breeds, "sheep-to-shawl" demonstrations (shearing, carding, spinning, knitting, and modeling, all on the spot and in an afternoon), and perhaps a business meeting of the association. Finally, nobody missed the barbecue of lamb on a grill accompanied by potluck salads, beans, desserts, and coffee and punch in paper cups, all served up on folding tables, under a big tent. There usually were printed handouts of favorite lamb recipes.

Our first year of lambing went by and I named all three of the lambs in our small flock. There was only one female, with two males in the first round of lambs. Feeling a little disappointed not to have more ewe lambs, we wethered the males to keep down the competition with the ram, considered the fate of males at auction, and decided we could support two more, even though ewe lambs are what you want for production.

The next year, I resolved not to name any "extra" males. I was sure I did not want to eat a lamb I knew by name. There were two. I tried not to learn their faces, merely to see them as anonymous white sheep, but of course they were recognizable. Inevitably, they became "Big No-name Lamb" and "Little No-name Lamb."

That was the year the barn collapsed in the big January windstorm—we had to build a new one. And the septic system went out and had to be replaced, and the pump failed on the well, and the price of sheep at auction dropped below cost. So much for coming out ahead. Bill was spinning as fast as he could—not like a top, but like a handweaver, since selling handwovens is one of the things he does. He's fast, but the fastest handspinner around can't use more than about a dozen fleeces in a year and still find time to change his socks. Moreover, our pasture won't support much more than a dozen sheep, even with the supplementary alfalfa and grain we feed them. One of the ram lambs looked good enough to sell for breeding, so I held out and named him. Adding the two no-names to our cottage-industry flock would make it fifteen. My husband called the local butcher in late November. Since then, we've been eating lamb.

And yet, I can't leave it alone, can't dismiss it without reflection. Here are some of the things I've been thinking about.

The Butcher

I pass the butcher's place on my way to work. His sign reads, "All American Butcher, Mobile Slaughtering"—which has always had a cruel, ironic sound to me, but the butcher isn't like that. He's an earnest, hard-working country man. The morning he came to get the lambs, he called and asked whether it was okay with us if he was a little late. "I hope it don't imposition you too much," he said, "but there's a man up to Forest Grove with a cow down and he wants to try and save her." To "save" in this case meant to kill and butcher the cow with an irreparably broken leg, before she died and became a "waste product."

Before we had the lambs butchered, I read a book about country women. One woman gave a long and moving account of her struggle in the sixties to go back to the land and survive. One of the skills she acquired was butchery. She related how two elderly bachelor brothers taught her the process, and how she would carry it out herself in a humane and useful way, taking the sacrificial sheep off to a remote part of the farm, giving it a pan of grain, and then killing it with a bullet through the head. The gist of the story was that anyone who eats meat ought to be able to kill it. Certainly the argument has some conviction. The country woman seemed responsible and worthy, and I believe it's good to live in awareness.

But I remember a friend, an ex-Green Beret, telling about his training days when he was given a knife and told to slit a goat's throat, the idea being that when you were fighting in the jungles of Asia you never knew when you might have to butcher your own dinner. Of course, once in the jungles of Asia, he realized there wasn't nearly as much chance of running into dinner as into the "enemy." The goat slaughtering exercise had been a way of breaking him in to spilling blood—and it worked, a fact perpetual and inescapable in his life ever since.

I'm not sure that every meat-eating human being should be a butcher. In my student on-the-road days, living for part of a year on the Greek island of Korfu, I noticed how differently food—and in particular, meat—was treated in the markets of Europe as compared to Oregon. At Christmas in Korfu town, huge beef carcasses hung, unrefrigerated, in the doors of meat stalls, the testicles, still attached to the carcass, decorated in red and green foil, the cavities of the carcasses decorated with greenery. I didn't eat much meat, mainly because I was living on less than a dollar a day for groceries, so a large part of my diet consisted of wild greens sold by peasant women along the street for two or three drachmas (about 10 cents). I would boil the greens, then lace them with the local olive oil, sprinkle with feta and lemon juice, and eat them with a chunk of fresh bread. But when I bought meat, about once a week, I would buy it from a nice young butcher named Tony whose open front stall was down the block from our apartment. One morning before I went out, I looked over the balcony of the apartment and saw a crowd gathered in front of Tony's shop. The police were there and I saw them lead Tony away in handcuffs. As it turned out, Tony's ex-girlfriend had come around with their child to protest his impending marriage to someone else. In the heat of argument, he had picked up a butcher knife and killed her as the child looked on. I think there must always be an element of danger in the butchery, in the sharpening of knives, the spilling of blood. Of course most butchers are non-violent, working people who take on a job the rest of us don't want to do, but it may be a good thing that not everyone is a butcher.

When I was a child during World War II, it was common for people to raise a few chickens to butcher. I remember going to buy chickens from a local farm and seeing them run around after the farmer had chopped off their heads. We children laughed and screamed and chased the headless bodies into the corn patch. The memory puzzles me, because I was always sentimental about animals, hated the mistreatment of pets, became nauseous at boys hunting robins with their BB guns, and yet my feelings did not extend to the chickens. Clearly something in my child-brain already had separated the named ones (individuals) from the nameless ones (meat). I was amazed at the headless running bodies, but lacking in pity, which surprises me now.

As to killing what I eat, my only prey so far has consisted of fish, crabs, and clams. I don't think I would be a competent butcher. If one is to eat meat, it makes sense to delegate the task to someone who can do it well and—I hope—humanely. The country woman with the gun seems an exception.

Religion

Since we butchered the two lambs (or rather, had them butchered), I have been thinking more about religion. I have been thinking about it with a recognition, which has never been so real to me before, that religion often employs the language of killing and eating meat as a central metaphor. I am most familiar with Christianity, and with the old and new testaments. "The next day he saw Jesus coming toward him, and said, 'Behold, the Lamb of God, who takes away the sin of the world!'" And "For the Lamb in the midst of the throne will be their shepherd, and he will guide them to springs of living water; and God will wipe away every tear from their eyes." Christ, of course, is the shepherd, but He is also the lamb. The baptized are washed in the blood of the lamb. Communion is a partaking of the body and blood of the lamb. Lamb and shepherd are one. The congregation is the flock. Eating and being eaten. The allegory of sacrifice is clear, and it is not merely symbolic. I appreciate the ancient knowledge that life is a cycle. The symbolism just doesn't have the same impact when you have been thinking of it only in terms of hamburger on a Styrofoam tray, reconstituted chicken balls, or shrink-wrapped wieners. Has meat become ridiculous in our time? What does it do to our values if we eat meat and think of it only as a packaged product?

Conservation

Eating our home-grown lamb, I am more careful than I have ever been not to waste. Each chop and roast and soup bone takes on an importance I had not considered before, must be appreciated. One cannot consider the perpetual flux of organisms being absorbed and transformed into one another without becoming a little dizzy. Or indignant, if you're of that mind—who invented this universe anyway? Why can't we live by eating rocks, nibbling the earth till we stand on a mole hill? All right, so we could live on corn and beans and Soya products. Someday I may make that choice and I will stop eating meat, but I have not come to that point yet.

In the meantime, I recognize as never before that the dinner I eat is not made of plastic and didn't originate in a box. It is a primitive and savage feeling, perhaps, but there is something balanced in it as well, realizing that the lamb you raised has become part of you. Imagine the responsibility, to carry in your living body the lives of other beings, to be given the gift of life sustained by life.

Live well. Conserve and treat with respect. Thank the lamb. You are the lamb.

Ambivalence

One night not long after we had the no-name lambs butchered, I woke up about 3 a.m. and lay there in the dark wondering what had awakened me. No dream. No sound. But with apparent randomness there in the dark I remembered a day last spring when the lambs were just a couple of weeks old and they had started to gambol. The whole bunch of them would run one direction as fast as they could, stop, pause a moment, turn around, and then run back again, back and forth, about fifty feet either way. After they had done this for a while they would stop and pant. It was comical and unexpected, to see lambs pant, like little dogs, or athletes, their heads down, their sides heaving. After they'd rested a while they would start all over. It was a scene I had forgotten, but out of nowhere it came back to me, clearly as a vision, in the middle of the night, at the beginning of December, the darkest month of the year.

The Gopher and the Gopher Snake

The first time I saw the snake in the garden it took my breath away. It was at least five feet long and thick as my wrist. I didn't know what kind of snake it was. Growing up on the west side of the Oregon Cascades, I was not worried about poisonous snakes, but the size of this one, slung out between the pale green leaves of the lettuce and the darker ones of the spinach, was startling. It was a tannish snake with brown lozenges of a darker color patterned in its scales. The snake hissed at the dog, who wagged his tail and looked interested. When we shooed the dog back, the snake hissed at us. "You are nothing," its hiss seemed to say. "You are air, and whistling, and a hollow space in the universe. Your bones are flutes for eternity and sand runs in your veins." Snakes are expert hissers. When it decided we'd been chastised long enough, it slid away. No hard feelings.

That was two years ago, our first gardening summer in the country. When we checked around we learned that it was a gopher snake—a benign, rodent-eating inhabitant of grass and woodlands—and we waited to see it again. We thought we did, a couple of times that first year, but perhaps it was a different snake. Once it seemed smaller, another time it seemed larger. Maybe there was more than one. In any case, the snake's habits kept it out of sight most of the time.

We were pleased to have a gopher snake around, because we seemed to have more than enough gophers. Their mounds of dirt came up in the most inconvenient places, in the middle of a row of purple onions, in the peas, in the patch of Yellow Finn potatoes. One morning sitting in bed drinking coffee and staring drowsily into the orchard, I saw a new Granny Smith apple tree start to jiggle. It shook, then trembled, was still for a moment, then shook violently. I called to Bill, "Something's got Granny Smith."

We went out to the yard and Bill took hold of the tree. It came out of the ground, rootless. The gophers had won again.

One thing about a gopher snake, you will notice immediately, is that its head is rather narrow, about the same width as its body. A snake is a no-neck being, and a gopher snake more than some. This, I imagine, makes it easy to slide down gopher holes and slurp up gophers. After the demise of our Granny Smith, I was more than ever hopeful of the well-being of our snake, which we had not seen for some time, though one day Bill saw a rubber boa (which I missed, regrettably), and we see the usual garter snakes and racers from time to time. Sometimes it seems I don't see snakes half as often as I did when I was growing up. I don't know if that's an effect of not being in the right place at the right time—something grownups suffer from—or something happening to the environment, but I'm interested in seeing snakes and take note when I do.

On the other hand, I wouldn't want to keep a snake for a pet. A friend has a boa constrictor and she claims that a robbery was once aborted at her house when the would-be robber saw the snake and fled. Another time, a different friend left a boa constrictor at our house for a few weeks while he broke the news to his new wife that he had a pet. Every once in a while he would come over and feed the snake a live rat, some time after which it would produce a large, hair-laced excretion, and that, so far as I could tell, was that. I couldn't blame the wife for holding off, but eventually the snake left our home and I lost track of how the menage worked out.

But wild snakes are something else. Outside the insect world there are no stranger, more alien beings, and yet they hold an eerie, attractive fascination. I think of Roethke's poem about a snake, his "wanting to be that form./And I may be, sometime." There are plenty of snake-haters, and there are folks who handle snakes and deem it a religious experience, and of course there's Medusa with her head full of snakes. Snakes are heavy duty on the archetypal side.

But I didn't care so much about all that. I just wanted my gopher snake back. I found myself in the garden on hot June days, midst gopher mounds and uprooted plants, muttering, "Come back snake, come back little gopher snake." Something not only was uprooting things but was eating the peas, vines and all, so Bill threw a piece of bird netting over the pea patch, which seemed to help.

Then, one day, as we were out in the garden to check the progress of the corn, I saw it. The gopher snake. It lay along the edge of the pea patch. I approached. But something was wrong. It did not hiss or raise its head. Its body convulsed but it did not slide off into the grass or turn and confront me. The snake had become entangled in the netting, and as its muscles flexed and contracted, the nylon mesh of the netting became more and more embedded in its scales. All along its five-foot length the snake was trapped by the constricting net. I tried lifting the net but the snake could not move, could not free itself.

I called Bill and we got a pair of scissors, but it seemed difficult to cut away the netting without damaging the snake's scales. Finally, after a certain amount of fumbling, we decided I would hold the snake and Bill would carefully, slowly, cut each thread of mesh that confined the snake. It hissed then, but with difficulty, as it attempted to move. I took hold of the snake's body with both hands, one behind its head and the other further down. Bill carefully began to snip away the netting. The gopher snake had become so entangled that the netting appeared to cut deep into its flesh, but as each thread was snipped, the snake seemed to recover. Finally, the last thread was severed, and I let him go. I could almost see him shake his scales into place like a dog after a bath or a goose after you've touched its feathers. The gopher snake gave one last hiss over its back and took off, sliding, apparently unhurt, into the grass.

We haven't seen the gopher snake since then, but I am hopeful of its well-being. As I let go of it, it gave off a terrible excretory smell, and though I washed my hands several times with every kind of sweet, deodorizing soap I could find in the house, my fingers still gave off that stench of angry snake. I can't say what the smell is like exactly, something stinking, something leadenly heavy as the smell of hot solder, something like certain plants that look sweet enough but smell bad when you crush their leaves. All that day I would find myself leaning my chin on a hand, reading a book, perhaps, and I would be distracted by a faint bad odor on my fingers and would have to go off to wash again.

Not long after my hand-to-coil encounter with the snake, we did have a curious sighting. Walking down the driveway with a painfully slow shuffle was a brown rodent of a sort we had never seen before. Not a squirrel, not a rat, not a mole, it seemed to have qualities of all three. The animal was about as large as a ground squirrel but a darker brown. When we approached it, it turned, stood up on its hind legs, and presented its open mouth. I don't know whether it was snarling or that was just the way it looked, but it had the longest front teeth I've ever seen on an animal that size—two long, yellow, top incisors, and shorter but nevertheless notable bottom ones. The animal had a naked tail like a rat, but it had ears so short and crumpled and insignificant they barely stood out from its head. On its front feet were big, pink, meaty paws, obviously digging instruments, like a mole's. Its eyes were beady little dark things the size of fish eggs. It was not the sort of fuzzy little creature of which one says, "Oh, Mommy, can I keep it?" We backed off a little, and it turned and began its way down the driveway again. Each time we approached to get a closer look, it reared up on its hind legs and looked so fierce we backed off. There was something so grim in its progress, it made us a little uneasy to find such a curious and unfriendly looking creature meandering down our driveway. We wondered if it was perhaps ill, and took care to keep the dogs away from it. Eventually it disappeared into the grass.

From a book on wildlife we later learned that we had encountered a pocket gopher, a common animal but one "rarely seen above ground." And a good thing, too, I thought. Was this small Grendel the creature that had been wreaking so much havoc in our garden? And if so, what was it doing going down the driveway and away from our place? And why had we simply stood there and watched it go? Should we not have waged war on it in some way, as the destroyer of our provender? And how many cousins and aunts and uncles had it left behind? Had the gopher snake, perhaps, swallowed the rest of its family?

I think about them from time to time, the moles, the roots, the grubs, the snakes, the gophers, the digging, the devouring, the dank chambers and tunnels and kingdoms of the sunless world. The smell of snake. But I live in the light above ground, and I cannot really imagine it, the dark ferocity of that subterranean life.

Drit

For a long time, the guy down at the corner, along the highway into town, had a sign out by the road that said: "Fill drit wanted." There is no end to inventive spelling in our county, such as when the feed store is advertising "chix, dux, & turx" for sale or offering to help with the Derby Days soap box race by providing "Way-In Here" on their industrial scale. I like to see such signs. They remind me of Shakespeare spelling his own name three different ways.

The "fill drit" sign was up for quite a while and it seemed to work. Every once in a while somebody would drive out with a pickup load of clay mixed with pieces of broken sidewalk or stumps and dump it on the guy's place. Then he'd spread it around a bit. We laughed about the "drit" and joked about getting our hands "dritty," then wondered whether drit was some country substance we didn't know about. But after several months his property rose up an inch or three out of the mud so I guess he knew what he was doing.

It had been kind of a wet place. At first he lived there in a trailer, but after he had raised the ground up a little he moved in an old mobile home and set it up on concrete blocks and the trailer disappeared. Then he put up a nice little A-frame pig house with a yard around it, moved in a couple of weaner pigs to raise, poured some big concrete posts that looked like something you'd tie the Queen Mary to, painted the tops of the concrete posts with glitter, like something from a 1957 prom, and strung fence wire between them. It looked like a regular mini-farm, as they call them in the real estate ads, and it was built on good old American *drit*.

Across the road on another place there was a little old trailer down in the marsh, and one day we noticed the guy on that place had put out a sign, "Fill dirt wamted." You know how you can get going on your "N's" and do one bump too many. Pretty soon the fellows with pickup loads of clay and sidewalk pieces and so on started dropping their loads on this guy's place. His ground got higher and higher too, just like the first guy's. After a while I guess this second guy had all the fill dirt he "wamted" because he took down the sign and turned to other things, like enclosing his trailer in wood and putting a roof over it. That project has been taking some time and we are interested to see how it will turn out. We are wondering whether the trailer will stay inside the wooden building or he will dismantle it piece by piece and carry it out the front door once the outside part is finished. To continue the Shakespearean association, this reminds me of a nice restaurant I once saw in England. They had cut a hole in the wall inside the building so that customers could see the original wattle structure of sticks and mud that had been the beginning of the building several hundred years earlier and all the layers that had been added since.

In the meantime, the guy who asked for "drit" moved in a double wide, and the other mobile home disappeared. So did the weaner pigs, which had gotten pretty big while this was going on. He also put up a mustard yellow, metal mini-barn, painted some rocks white, and arranged them around his petunias. Bill said, mysteriously, that the painted rocks meant the guy must have been in the army.

The guy on the opposite side who "wamted" dirt, when not working at enclosing his trailer in plywood, began collecting old tractors which he arranged on the dirt fill that now lined the creek that runs through his property. But so far he has not planted petunias in the tractors or painted any rocks. I suspect that may happen, though, as there seems to be no end to the home improvement game.

It must be a challenge to stare across the highway and the creek at your neighbor's property gradually rising higher than yours, and then satisfying to gaze from yours rising higher than his. One guy asked for drit and the other wamted dirt and they got the same thing—elevation.

Now another example of the territorial imperative has caught my attention.

When Bill and I went out for a walk recently I noticed the milk bottle fiend had added another quarter-mile or so of milk bottles to his fence posts. This is up in the hills from our place. We like to drive a ways and then get out and hike with the dogs. We hadn't been to the mountain of the milk bottle fiend for several months, but you could see he'd been drinking a lot of milk since we were there last.

We don't know who the milk bottle fiend is, but when we first noticed the plastic gallon jugs they seemed to lead to and up a particular driveway, so we thought we knew where he lived—until our recent walk, when I noticed upended milk jugs on the metal T-posts that lined a second driveway down the road and opposite. A relative maybe? A competitor? A victim of style? Hard to tell.

The jugs are the big, plastic, gallon-size, white ones. There are hundreds of them along the roads up there in the woods, hundreds of plastic milk jugs upended on the tops of metal fence posts. We have tried to guess the meaning of this display. It doesn't seem colorful or kinky enough to be folk art. And it seems too permanent and extensive to be intended as a guide to a family picnic, such as the paper plates or colored balloons you sometimes see along a country road, nailed up on telephone poles, and which hang there disintegrating for months after the McPherson family reunion or Mary Helen's baby shower is over.

Much of the land surrounded by these milk jug-topped fenceposts is rough grazing ground, and whoever owns the place runs a few cattle on the grass between the scrub oak and Scotch broom plants. This leads me to wonder whether the bottles are intended to scare off wandering deer and elk that might compete with the cattle—and whether it works. I can almost picture some wild old farmer up there in the hills living entirely on milk just so he can secure his holdings.

We have conjectured that the milk bottles are some sort of warning, echoing, for instance, the severed-head motif in Romanesque churches, a remnant of pre-Christian Celtic practices. I read an article that claimed the knobs on porch banisters are a modern version of the ancient practice of nailing one or more skulls at the entrance of one's home in order to ward off danger. If banister knobs, why not milk cartons?

I think the cartons look like kind of a mess, but I don't intend to interfere so long as they're not on my fence. You never know what might be behind a couple of miles of T-posts topped with upside-down milk cartons, marching along the road like gallon-sized skulls.

The Goose Chronicles

$$\textcircled{\tiny{\wp}}$$

What prompted me to get a pair of goslings I'm not sure. Some vague ideal, perhaps an image of wild geese from childhood: the chilly, immaculate distance between an autumn sky and the wandering mind, a blade of grey wing across the marbled moon. Or maybe it was some odd Alsation gene on my mother's father's side, inherited memories of a sturdy pair of hands fondling the force-fed gorge, fattening the sweet liver, hands full of plucked down. One imagines a stone doorsill leading to the kitchen garden, the gleam of light on feathers and the amusing perambulations of the flock in the summer garden. A glass of white wine on a garden table catching the golden autumn light. Certainly, reading Selma Lagerlof's *The Wonderful Adventures of Nils*, a book about a boy who shrinks and travels with a flock of wild geese, impressed my childhood. On the one hand, geese meant wild beauty; on the other they were a comfortable and beautiful element in a well-ordered country landscape. I also had heard them described as barnyard guards, slug police, and garden weeders.

At the feedstore I studied the demonstration posters on the wall for half an hour. There were bright pictures of all kinds of geese: Toulouse, Embden, Pilgrim, Chinese, Pomeranian, African, and Dewlapped. The place had a wonderful smell of grain and dust and the forest-scented cedar chips sold for animal bedding. The floor was made of heavy fir boards worn by fifty years of farm boots, and everywhere I looked there was stuff to *use*. Woven wire and horse tack, dog biscuits and hoof trimmers, hummingbird feeders and Ivamec vermifuge, denim jackets and chicken waterers, rose food, and nested sizes of feed dishes in eight different colors of bright plastic so strong you could drop one out of a jumbo jet at thirty thousand feet and it wouldn't break. I love feedstores. I wasn't in a hurry to leave. After studying the pictures and descriptions, I finally ordered two grey Africans, a goose and a gander.

It wasn't long till the spring stock of geese, ducks, and chicks arrived and I was able to pick up my pair—little peepers I could cup in my hands—and take them home in a beer carton supplied by the feedstore. Their baby plumage was a grayish yellow, almost olive green, and they had dark bills and feet. Because they were hatchery birds, they required the protection of a heat lamp until they began to grow feathers and to develop an oily waterproof coating for their plumage—something they would have gotten from nestling under their mother had they been naturally hatched. I kept them in a large, newspaper-lined box in the sunroom, with a hot orange light dangling from an improvised hook mounted on the back of a chair.

As usual when I undertook the care of any new creature, the dark side rose up to haunt me. I would wake early in the morning wondering whether they had survived the night, rush to the box, and find them happily pecking feed and messing up their water dispenser, a circular red plastic apparatus that attached to the mouth of an upside-down Mason jar. Happily, the young geese did well.

As they quickly grew and became too large, raucous, and messy for the sunroom, I moved them to the laundry room, which had a door that opened into the back yard. During the day they would forage outside, then at night make their way back into their box in the laundry room. As with all growing beings, they gradually became more independent, and as the weather warmed up I began to leave them out at night. I tried briefly to pen them with the chickens, but any effort to move them to the chicken enclosure met with honking and wing flapping and general resistance. The pair soon convinced me that confinement was the last thing they wanted, so eventually I let them roam at will.

For a pond I got them a yellow plastic wading pool with blue pictures of Smurfs in the bottom (a discount store special), and they spent many happy days drinking and dunking their heads, washing their eyes and dribbling water down their necks. In the water they would ruffle their feathers and spread themselves low in the shallow pool, fluttering and throwing water in bright arcs onto the lawn.

I gave them all the fresh water I could, though we were having a drought year. The newspapers were full of it and there was a restriction on yard watering in nearby Portland. We didn't need an official restriction as we were on our own rural low-capacity well, and when it ran out, it ran out. But to conserve, I filled their plastic pond with fresh water every few days, and when it became dirty, dumped the water onto the nearby bed of daylilies which seemed to flourish with this treatment. Thus our scarce water did double duty.

Water was so attractive to the geese—it was clearly a source of health and well-being. As they grew older, it also aroused their amorous instincts. After a vigorous bath, they would retire to the lawn and mate, she modestly arching her neck and pretending diffidence, he treading her delicately and waving his wings like a feathered tornado. Then, with him hooting and elaborately parading and her sighing and elegantly fluttering her feathers into place, they would resume their march around the farm, plumage sleek, eyes bright, body and soul satisfied. He was obviously mad about her.

The following spring I found an egg in the driveway—it had apparently been an unplanned egg. But not long after, they began to gather dried grass and leaves into an uneven little mound just inside the crawl space of the house. Definitely a plan. One day there was an egg in the nest. Next there were two, and so on, until there were ten large eggs and she began to sit. For a whole month she stayed there, only occasionally getting up to stretch her legs, but never did she go more than a foot or two away from the nest and never did she stray off it for more than a few minutes. The geese ate a variety of greens and bugs as well as the daily ration of grain we gave them, but their main food was tender green grass. I was concerned that the nesting goose was not able to browse. I moved a pan of water near her and left small offerings of food, but she seemed to eat little.

In the meantime, the gander had become quite distant. It was a ruse, of course. All that month he patrolled the area at the edge of the back yard, never going near the nest but always maintaining a set distance from it, about thirty feet, walking round and round as if he and his lady were, like Donne's lovers, two points of a compass, she the stationary, he the roving one.

At the end of May the eggs began to hatch. It took three or four days for eight goslings to struggle out of their shells. Now the gander returned to his love and their new family. With peeping offspring there was no more chance that the goose would escape the notice of passing predators; the gander took up a protective stance close by, between them and the rest of the world.

For another day the goose and gander lingered over the nest, then decided the remaining two eggs were a lost cause and abandoned them. I was curious, so I cracked one and found it was still just an egg, yolk and white; it had been infertile. Except for being slightly thick in appearance it actually looked "fresh." A bluejay broke the other but no one seemed to care because by now the goose and gander were into touring the farm with their goslings. All day they marched up hill and down, eating grass, snipping off seed heads with gusto, digging around the roots of shrubs where leaf mulch might hide slugs and bugs, and generally enjoying life's feast. Goose and gander returned to bathing in their yellow plastic pond, and soon the little ones tried it and liked it.

For a while when the goslings were small the whole family returned each evening to the niche under the house. There they would be safe, out of the way of owls and foxes, though one evening I heard the geese honking as if disturbed and a hooting sound from the tree above the deck. I went out to find a horned owl looking down from a dead branch in the oak tree, obviously checking out supper. At my appearance it flew away and the goslings settled comfortably under their mother's broad wings. The gander stood guard.

Another small near-mishap occurred one day when they were parading through the walnut grove. They habitually marched with dad in front, followed by the eight peepers, followed by mom in the rear. One moment there were eight, the next I counted seven. I went out to the tall grass to see where the other had gone, snatched by a snake perhaps or a stray cat. (Our own cats would never have dared come near the gander and goose. They had had too many encounters already and were wary of head bonks and powerful wing flappings.) I couldn't find gosling number eight until I stood there a few minutes and finally heard a misplaced peeping. Parting the grass, I saw him in the bottom of an old post hole, into which he had dropped from life's parade. I reached down and pulled him out. A great family celebration took place—honks, peepings, sighs, squawks—and then the parade resumed.

I never actually named the geese, though over time I came to think of the father as Grandgousier, a character from Rabelais. For some reason, the mother became Madame Goosoolias. Except that I liked the sound, there was no justification for the French character of their names—I had ordered Africans, after all. But as they grew up they failed to take on the large knob and dewlap of the Africans and were generally more delicate and swanlike. They developed smallish knobs but no dewlap to speak of, just a slight pouch under the bill. A look at some reference books told me that what I had were more likely Brown Chinese. Nevertheless, African or Chinese, I felt their aggressive, stylish, bon vivant character was essentially French, even Rabelaisian, so Grandgousier and Madame Goosoolias they remained.

Letting them have the run of the place created some small problems—droppings on the walk outside the house, for one thing.

They also developed the habit of snitching cat food, which we kept for our cats outside the kitchen door. The cats were completely undone by any advance from a goose. We moved the cat food to a table out of reach, but still the geese liked to march to the back door, sip from the watering bowl we left there for the cats and dogs, and honk loudly, standing on tiptoes and fixing their beady black eyes on the window as if they thought we ought to be bringing COB, the molasses-flavored corn-oats-barley mixture all the animals seem to love. We hosed off the sidewalk on a daily basis, shooed the geese back into the pasture (whose fence they somehow always seemed able to get out of but never back into), and tried to resist being conditioned to provide COB on command.

If they had known that reward is part of the conditioning process, they might have been more successful in upping their COB ration because we were always generous. A bucket full of COB on its way to a pan in the pasture brought the geese honking and swaying from side to side as they accompanied us to the preferred feeding place, but as soon as one of us dumped the grain into the pan, the father would turn and warn us off, beating his wings, stretching out his neck, and running at us with bad-tempered hisses, as if we might steal it back again. I tried to explain to him that reward, not punishment, creates desired behavior, but he never seemed to understand.

Leaving an encounter with a cranky goose requires a certain strategy. For one thing, you never turn your back—it looks as if you're running away. The retreating backside of any other entity looks, to a goose, like something to chase and bite. Like a peasant before a king in the great hall, you always back away, and if he stretches out his neck as if to bite or chase, you pause humbly, to signify you mean no harm, till he settles down.

I sometimes have asked myself, can a goose really discriminate to the extent that it recognizes that people, like geese themselves, have both a front and a back? It's a little difficult for me to imagine a goose seeing us human beings so articulated, having arms, legs, eyes, voices, fronts, backs, etc. One might expect a goose to see a human being merely as a large, mobile blob of COB-delivering protoplasm. How does a goose discriminate? (Sheep, by the way, are said not to care about the difference between the front and back of a human being. They are interested mainly in which direction you're moving, whether you're facing them or not.) I can only guess that for a goose it is the face that signals "front," but even there my mind boggles. After all, if attacked from behind by a goose I may turn and look at the goose without completely turning around, but that doesn't stop the goose in any way. I have to turn and "face" the goose with my whole body before he stops chasing me. It works, but standing up to a goose this way produces a not entirely satisfying reaction. The goose stops, retreats a few steps, honks rather shrilly on the upper end of the goose scale, turns, flaps his wings, and pretends to have been walking in the opposite direction all the time, albeit on tiptoe to look taller, and with his own rear slightly tucked so as not to be bitten by the "enemy."

Having thus dissuaded the gander from attacking you and pinching *your* unprotected rear—particularly the soft back of your leg—with a sharp bite, you turn and go on your way, but then the whole crowd of geese will stand tall over their COB, honking and shrieking, flapping their wings in what is clearly a victory celebration, as if it were their collective will, not yours, that ruled the day.

Dealing with a goose reminds me of teasing games children sometimes play to get under each other's skin: one of them says something and the other immediately remarks, "I wanted you to say that," ad infinitum. Or, "I'm rubber, you're glue. Whatever you say bounces off of me and sticks to you." One thing you soon learn in dealing with geese is that, from the goose's point of view, the goose always wins. A goose is always rubber.

My father found my geese amusing. A photographer, he was always trying for the perfect picture, and he tried many times to get a good picture of our geese. The goose and the goslings showed no particular interest in communicating with my father, but the gander always approached him in a high ceremonial manner, lifted on tiptoes, head straight up, the neck extended and beak straining upward to look as tall as possible. The beak pointed heavenward but the eyes rolled in his head to stay fixed on my father from this strained and elevated position. Thus Grandgousier would approach. Once the gander arrived at my father's feet he assumed a different sort of posture. Arching his neck and looking down at the ground, he would make mincing steps back and forth, swaying his neck like a snake, then take my father's pants leg in his beak and tug. Then, sighing a breathy little whistle, the gander would turn the other way and approach, again sidling up to my father and tugging on his trousers. Following that he would march around with his neck once more stretched toward the sky, his wings half extended. Then my father would take his picture. Sometimes, just to get the gander riled, my father would reach out and lightly pinch his beak. When he got a chance, the gander would reach back and pinch my father's hand, then my father would reach for the gander's neck and the gander would prance around, pull again on my father's pants leg and so on, but there was little of the wild display that seemed to mean the gander wanted to chase someone off. Instead, the gander always seemed happy to see my father, who visited every couple of months or so. Always the bird went through the same routine of mincing steps, half-extended wings, hootings and sighings and graceful extensions of his neck, either straight upward or in a swanlike arch. It always seemed that the gander recognized my father and was glad to see him. Once in a while, when my father had been especially teasing, the gander would respond with a tough bite and break the skin on the back of my father's hand. Then Dad would come in the house and say, "Look what your goose did!" and make a rueful face, but I felt they understood one another in some mild troublemaking way. I would bring my father a bandage and some antibiotic, along with a shot of whiskey to ease the pain, but it didn't mean he wouldn't tease the gander again.

Goose life went along smoothly with the goslings growing into young geese. It was not clear to me which were females and which males, but there were clearly some who displayed more "feminine" posture (the arched neck and mild looks of the mother) and more masculine behaviors (the broad-breasted, wing-flapping hooting challenges of the father), so I gradually sorted them out, guessing at best. To "sex" a goose, you have to hang onto it, flip it on its back, and go through a series of intrusive maneuvers bound to rile any creature. It didn't seem worth the trouble.

When they were eight or nine months old and about the same size as their parents, the offspring still were very much under the tutelage and guardianship of the adults, maintaining their middle position in marches across the field, though they did not always seem to have the manners of their parents, occasionally batting their wings at the dad and clustering a few feet away hooting rudely when father goose made his evening sighs and squawks as supplications for COB. Sometimes company would ask how we could stand the noise, but actually the geese made the most noise whenever company arrived. Other times they were quiet for hours except for the small, pleasant sounds one could only call sighs, a low musical exhalation of breath on a declining note, which they made as they went about their grass-plucking or settled into a resting flock.

It seems geese don't sleep much. Certainly they are light sleepers. I think they are watchful at night, but during the daytime after a good feed they often gather in a close formation, each standing on one foot, their heads tucked under their wings, and appear to sleep. Other times they actually sit down on the grass to tuck their heads away, thus resembling a cluster of grey stones on the lawn. Whatever they do, they all seem to do it at once and in more or less the same direction.

I never had a sick goose, and I wondered at their remarkable resistance to disease and infection, particularly considering the masses of dirt and grit that passed through their guts. Besides eating grass and bathing, our geese enjoyed digging up mouthfuls of mud and tossing it into their wading pool, and they sometimes uprooted plants and did the same thing. I don't know why, unless it was an effort to convert the plastic wading pool into something more natural and weedy-bottomed. But when the pool got clogged with mud, weeds, gravel, and goose droppings, they would bathe in it but seem not to enjoy it so much. Then I dumped the pool out and refilled it with clean, clear water. This always brought on wild goose celebrations, so I know they enjoyed the clean stuff.

A couple of times our male border collie, Jack, bit the gander on the bill. Jack tolerated the geese up to a point but he clearly didn't like them. They always hooted and threatened him with hisses, and as a macho-type dog he only put up with this because we insisted. The time when Jack snapped back and drew blood, the gander had bitten Jack's tail when Jack was trying his best to walk away and still maintain dignity. Even so, the gander seemed to recover without any evident infection of the small wound.

Besides chasing the dog, another bad habit the geese indulged in got one of them in serious trouble one morning. In winter when the ditches along our road were full of weeds and water, they would do whatever they could to slip through or over a weak spot in the fence to enjoy these natural pools. Once on the road, however, they got distracted with stopping cars. I sometimes wakened to cars honking and came out to see the geese with wings outspread facing the grill of a Ford 350 pickup or a delivery truck from the mushroom plant down the road. What touching, fragile, foolhardy machismo. We tried to keep them in, but they were devious and determined. One day someone didn't stop. We found one of the geese with its foot flattened by a car tire. He couldn't walk, so we carried him back to the yard. Meanwhile, we were being wingbeaten and pecked at by the rest of the crowd, who were determined to protect their wounded brother. We questioned whether he should be put out of his misery, but as he seemed quiet and content to merely sit, and because he was willing to eat food and drink water, we left him sitting on a grassy spot near the chicken house to see if he might improve. For almost two weeks the others stood in attendance, not deserting him for a minute. We carried food to all of them and they made do with whatever grass was at hand, though it must have been tempting to march out into the lush spring pasture and never look back. They were supremely defensive of the injured goose. I was amazed at their animal loyalty. After a few days the invalid began to stand on the uninjured leg, but he had difficulty in hopping so he didn't go far. In a week he began to put the injured foot down and then hop awkwardly, dragging it. After a couple of weeks he moved awkwardly down the field with the others surrounding him protectively, but he didn't go far. After that it appeared he would live but be lame. He was generally behind the others and walked with an extreme limp, as if the injured leg had healed shorter than the other. But after two months of steady improvement, it became impossible for us to tell which animal had been the injured one. I later learned that we should have splinted the leg by pulling it straight out and taping it to a popsicle stick or some such brace to help it heal right, but in this case we were lucky, and even without that treatment the leg healed more completely than we could have imagined. I hoped that this warning would keep them out of the road, but I doubted that would be the case when the winter rains came again and filled the ditches with tempting water and weed.

When winter came, I worried that I should shelter our geese at night to keep their knobs from freezing, but again they resisted all efforts to confine them to the chicken house, setting up such a honk and squall the chickens were totally miserable as well, and beating a retreat to the gate every time we opened it. I let them return to the barnyard. Our winters are fairly mild, but still we have occasional snowstorms. One night I looked out into the yard to see the geese under the yard lamp, snowflakes blowing at an angle across the yard. The geese were standing with their necks thrust into the slanting snow. It was as if they were imagining flying into the storm. They stretched out to meet it, an image of goose ecstasy.

Ten was a lot of geese, but I gave a friend who admired them a pair of the young ones, leaving us with six yearlings and the two originals. They made a pretty flock, meandering uphill and down snipping at the grass and picking slugs off the daffodils that had begun to sprout at the end of winter, themselves looking like little green goose heads coming out of the chilly, wet ground.

When winter passed and March arrived with all its flowers, we woke one morning to find a dead goose in the yard. It was one of the young females. Her shoulder had been bitten and she had been tossed and dragged across the walnut grove, then left there. We buried the goose near the lilac hedge and kept an eye out for interlopers.

A few weeks later we woke to find the mother goose and one of the other females dead in the yard, similarly chewed and tossed around, and the third, last female, missing. I followed a trail of feathers through the oak woods along the road, but found nothing more. (This was when I called the neighbors and asked whether their dog had brought home a dead goose. They said they'd check but they were sure he hadn't.) I had seen a bobcat running through the woods earlier that winter, so I had to concede that the attack might have been a wild animal—though they are inclined to grab just one and take off with it, whereas a domestic dog will kill geese and chickens and toss them around. There was no one to answer for the loss of the geese.

It was probable that the dog or whatever it was that took our geese had picked on the females because they were less aggressive than the males. Now we were left with the father and four sons. For a while the father seemed definitely dispirited. He was nervous and honky and inclined to bite and flap his wings at just about anything that moved. He was clearly determined to defend "the boys," and I imagined him waiting for the return of his dear lost goose wife, determined to take care of things on his own till she returned. A gander may enjoy three or four wives, but that does not mean he is not loyal. He is, intensely so. The death of a mate may bring on mourning and death. Our gander at least continued to eat and wander in the company of his sons as he looked for his dear one. Alas, nevermore.

Even though the young ganders were getting to be bigger than he was, he continued to act as if they were little goslings in need of his protection. He would honk for COB, and when I delivered it in a pan in the barnyard he would step between me and the boys, flapping his wings and keeping a wary eye lest I disturb their meal. While they greedily downed the grain, he took not a bite until they appeared satisfied. If one of the dogs came near, he again threw himself between the dog and the goslings—now grown into big, gaggling ganders.

I missed the elegant symmetry of the original pair. Friends suggested that domestic geese were meant to be dinner, that we should get Grandgousier another lady and eat the boys. Moreover, goose droppings on the walk to the kitchen door were not appealing. The ganders were noisy, ungrateful, alarming to small children, messy, and as to weeding the garden, they were more apt to pull up the peas and leave the grass.

My father still enjoyed visiting the gander, and when Dad arrived, the gander would revive his interest in the old games, go through his greetings and posturing, and in general have a good time. None of the "boys," by contrast, ever showed an interest in striking up an acquaintance with my dad; they were standoffish and wary. I imagined the menage as a good father of the old school, the kind who does what needs to be done, and his gaggle of hillbilly sons, each more uncouth than the other.

The next spring my father came to visit and again, in his walks about the place, he teased the gander. The gander marched around and honked and, more deferentially than usual, pulled on the legs of my father's trousers, as if to tell him how hard life had become now that he was left with these boys to raise all by himself. My father commiserated. They had a good visit.

My father wasn't feeling well that spring and so his visit wasn't long. Before he left, he was sitting on the front porch enjoying the view of the Coast Range and drinking his coffee, well dosed, as always, with cream and sugar. The geese paraded past.

"You ought to keep those geese," my father said out of the blue. "They're good guard geese. Don't get rid of them."

That was just before my father's cancer returned. He never came back to our house again. He spent the summer saying good-bye at the house where he and my mother lived on the southern Oregon coast. We went to see him several times. All his children and various grandchildren and a lot of other people who knew and loved him also showed up to visit one last time. He moved fragilely into the sun-filled yard, with the hummingbirds he loved so much coming and going among the fuchsias and geraniums. Sometimes he would walk out to the porch and sit on a chair, working to draw one more breath, until he was too weak for that. He died at the end of July.

I miss my father a lot. He was one of the most interesting people I've ever met. He was a photographer and all my life I associated him with the smell of photo chemicals and the darkroom. There are few sounds so peaceful to me as the gentle slosh of a picture being rocked back and forth in the developing tray under the warm glow of a safelight, my father staring at the print coming up on the paper, whistling softly under his breath, not a real whistle but something almost like a sigh, some fragmentary little melody almost beyond the human ear. He was also a pilot and for years he combined his two loves by taking aerial photos for a living, sometimes hiring a plane but usually flying himself in the old Piper J3, sometimes with the door off so that he could fly with one hand and lean out of the plane and take pictures with the other.

I didn't have to keep the geese. I knew that. They really were messy, loud, and ungrateful. But they were pretty to look at and had a lot of family feeling. I don't think I've ever seen an animal so devoted to family. When the old gander came up to me, sidling that way, as if he'd just as soon bite as not, and gave me a look with these mild, beady little eyes of his, I wondered: was he always looking for a handout or was he sometimes just looking for company? I imagined him looking at me and wondering: *Think my goose is ever coming back? These boys here are a handful. And whatever happened to that guy who used to come around here, the one with the camera?*

One day last fall, about three weeks before Christmas, we had a windstorm. I was in the city having lunch with my sister and my son. People kept warning us that there was a big storm on the way, but the air seemed calm and mild. I had a haircut appointment and I wanted to get a start on Christmas shopping before finals week at the college, when I would most certainly be tied down grading papers. We ate at a middle-eastern restaurant, wonderful plates of hummus and falafel, yoghurt dip, olives, pita bread, steaming bowls of lentil soup, a glass of hot sweet tea. We talked and dallied. It seemed I would have plenty of time to get home. By the time we finally left the restaurant, the wind had arrived. I started driving south out of town. It was forty miles to the farm. Just as I was leaving the crowded downtown, the power went out. Without traffic lights, the crush of people leaving work and trying to get home before the storm turned into a massive traffic jam. Tree branches started flying overhead. Electric wires were down. At one point, no doubt foolishly, I drove under a tree leaning across a net of utility cables. I just wanted to get home. Four hours later I arrived. Bill came anxiously out to meet me. He had been, understandably, worried. On the battery-operated radio he had heard that a woman not far from our place had been killed in her car by a falling tree. Other people were hurt or stranded. We had lost one of the big trees but it hadn't hit any wires or buildings going down. There was no other serious damage so far. Our power was off so the well was down, but earlier Bill had drawn off drinking water and had made a fire in the woodstove. Candles were flickering on the kitchen table. I was grateful to be home, but even as I climbed from the car and ran for the house I noticed a quiet under the sound of wind rushing through oak branches. Bill had put the sheep in the barn, the chickens had gone to roost in the early dark, the cats and dogs were all in, but where were the geese?

We never did find those geese.

The next day, after the storm, we searched our twenty acres, expecting to find our geese, or at least their bodies, in the woods or in the lower pasture. Not so much as a feather. We drove up and down the roads nearby and listened on the wind for the sound of goose calls, which we knew from experience could be heard for miles. Nothing. We went farther afield, looking and listening for a father gander and four big boys. I even called the county animal shelter but they said they didn't deal with geese. It's been quite a while now, but when I drive by geese foraging in a pasture I still study them to see whether they look like our lost geese. They never do.

Our geese were too heavy, too domestic, to really fly. At best they could lift themselves three or four feet off the ground and coast downhill from the barn to the bottom of the pasture. Sometimes when there was a breeze they would spread their enormous wings and get a little lift. You could tell they liked it, but it didn't last long. I imagine them that day of the big wind, spreading their wings and facing into the southwest where the wind came from. I imagine the father gulping big drafts of sea air from over the Coast Range and taking a run for it. I imagine his big, heavy-bodied boys following him. I wonder what they found. I wonder how high they went.

Horse

I woke to see the sunrise red between the tail end of Chehalem mountain and the rain clouds forming above it, a scarlet glimpse of possibility. It was November. As I sat up in bed, peering out at the dawn, I saw an unfamiliar silhouette in the vineyard. Just at the crest of the hill where the slope goes down toward the lower field, there was a spotted horse.

In seconds, as the day grew lighter, I saw that it was in fact an appaloosa, with a grey and white spotted rump and wearing a saddle. I called Bill to look, and we went out to the vineyard, he taking a rope to throw over its neck, if possible. The horse was calm enough seeing him coming, but when Bill tried to throw a rope around its neck, it took off into the vineyard following a trail Bill had mowed with the tractor into the scrub oak at the border of the property. The horse came to the end of the trail and stood there, again calmly, until the dogs came out and began to bark. Bill ordered the dogs back to the house, hollering at Jack, who then got down on his belly and begged for forgiveness, while the horse took off running uphill this time, heading for the oak grove behind the barn. There it stopped, but would not be approached without showing a nervous inclination to run off again, so we left it.

Bill called the sheriff and two men came out to see if they could tell, by the way the horse was "got up," whether it appeared to have thrown someone who might be lying out along the roads or pastures somewhere. A horse had been reported missing along Ridge Road, but it didn't fit this description. The sheriff's men determined this horse had not been bridled and then left.

A while later a red pickup appeared to be slowly making a search along the ridge on the other side of the valley. I jumped into the car and drove that way to ask them whether they were looking for a horse, but as I came to the end of Coyote Lane the truck left the road and took off across a field. It soon was out of sight, so I returned home.

The horse now seemed to have settled into the oak grove, so we let it be. I sat out on the porch with my coffee, peeling apples for a pie. I left the two border collies inside where they sat pressing their noses against the screen and rolling their eyes alternately at me and at the horse on the hill. They clearly thought something ought to be done. I'm kind of scared of horses. I've never been around them and they seem unmanageably large. I've known a couple of horse-loving friends who had to go around for a while with bandages on their broken noses after walking behind a familiar horse, and Bill has a story about rolling with a horse that took a spill in the south coast dunes before I knew him. I do remember wanting a horse when I was nine or ten, wanting to *be* a horse I think, imagining that nothing could be better than to run like that, with all that hide and muscle.

I was starting to fantasize about having a horse, maybe this one, when the red pickup returned and Bill waved it down. The man and woman in the truck indeed were out looking for the horse. Someone had tried to ride the horse the night before—they said he'd tried three times and been thrown off three times before the horse ran away.

"'I don't think that's the horse for you, Bub,' I told him," said the man in the truck as his wife went off up the hill, with a bridle, to coax the horse back. "That horse don't like men," he continued, "just women. He'd been abused when we got him. I got him off Hollis Taylor, that I get my wild horses from."

The woman coaxed the horse out of the oak grove with a can of oats, offering them in her hand. Then she slipped the bridle on him and brought him down the hill to us. "Looks like he got a gash," she said, with a glance at the horse's hind leg, where a rectangular patch of skin the size of a Hershey bar was missing. The horse began to roll his eyes and skitter a little. "There, there, Son," said the woman. She offered another handful of oats. "That's all right, Son, just take it easy there."

I did not know if the horse's name was Son, or if this was her affectionate way of calming the horse. Her voice was throaty, melodious and soothing like some country and western singers. She had beautiful sad eyes and sharp, high cheekbones. "Don't get riled, Son. Just take it easy there. Just go slow, Son."

The man introduced himself to Bill as I looked on from the porch. He said, "We bought that piece down Goodrich road." Bill told him we'd looked at the place. The man said, "Just about got that sheep barn cleaned up. Whooee. What a mess. Been there about six months. Got a pig started."

Bill said, "Oh you do."

The man said, "Yup, going to litter any day now."

The woman proceeded to lead the horse down the road, walking him home. The man got into the truck and drove away. I sat on the porch and stared after them, the man with the pig started, the woman with the voice, and Son, the appaloosa who didn't like men. I sat on the porch for another hour or so, waiting to see what else might come down the road, and I didn't go in till it started to rain.

Water

When we bought Lilac Hill Farm, it was put to us as a great advantage that there were six wells on it. We should have realized what that meant. One good well is all you really need on twenty acres. Six wells meant six tries at getting a good one. And only one of the five was actually hooked up to the house and operating. The others were mysterious holes in the ground in which a dropped pebble gave a distant *plunk* and was gone.

It's not that there wasn't any water. It was there, and when the house well went dry and the circuit breaker cut off you could switch it on again after a brief wait. The main house well was 220 feet deep, but the composition of the soil was such that water flowed through it slowly. We soon found that a sprinkler in the garden for forty minutes meant the well emptied, the system shut off, and it would be half an hour before we could flip the reset and take even a glass of drinking water again. Two extra house guests taking long showers over a weekend could mean timeout of a day or more on laundry and dishes, if not total shutdown.

The previous owners hadn't mentioned this of course. They blithely waved the well report, filed at the time the most recent well was dug, nine years earlier, in 1978. The report showed a small but adequate flow, seven gallons per minute. Five gallons per minute was required for a bank loan. Without that well report, we could not have gotten our mortgage.

After the pump kept shutting off I studied the report, wondering what was wrong. It looked legal and impressive. The drilling company had testified to a "Bailer test" of "7 gal./min. with 157 ft. drawdown after $1^1/_2$ hrs." There were all the reassuring figures and the descriptions of various strata of soil, the very language intimating mysterious and ancient geologic events: *Topsoil from zero to two feet down. Brown and yellow decomposed clay to fifteen feet. Firm Gray shale with layers of white limestone to 178 feet. Very hard shale with layers of gray and brown limestones, volcanic ash, and caving conditions to two hundred seven feet. Firm Gray shale to 220 feet.* At 220 feet was the mysterious bottom of our well. It was cased all the way down, with perforated pipe from 180 to 220 feet to allow water to flow into the cavity. Although the casing was six inches in diameter down to twenty feet, after that it was only four inches. The temperature of the water, which had first been found at 106 feet, was fifty-one degrees, and the static level after the well was drilled was fifty-eight feet below the surface. Fascinating. I took this to mean that when the well was full we should have about 150 to 160 feet of water in a four-inch-wide tube. I had forgotten much of my high school geometry, but I imagined 160 four-inch-wide two-liter cola bottles sitting on top of one another. It would be a lot of Pepsi but not a lot of water. Still, the important thing was whether the well would refill at a fast rate. When the whole earth is your sponge, what does a well casing signify? Sometimes, we discovered, quite a lot.

There had been several dry years in the West. People blamed it on El Niño, the warm current that sometimes shifted capriciously offshore, changing the location of the Gulf Stream, the temperature of the ocean, and with it the weather. The year we bought the place, *Jean de Florette* was a popular French movie and its message was like a knife in the heart. City folks trying to live in the country—a dangerous business. So far as I could tell there weren't any hidden springs on our place. Still, I wondered whether water scarcity was something recent related to the drought or whether it was a chronic problem in the area. I started thinking about the flow of water. This was western Oregon, after all—land of rivers and rain jokes. There couldn't be a water shortage here.

Wrong.

My brother, a geologist, tells me that depending on the soil involved, it could take a hundred years for a theoretical drop of rainwater hitting the ground to make its way down to 220 feet, depending on the permeability of the sand, clay, stone, and so on. He said there probably was plenty of water down there in terms of just our use, though we were apparently not on an easily tapped aquifer. What we were getting was a slow trickle of water oozing through the deep earth. We have few neighbors and no major industrial wells nearby. Unlike the fast developing Parrett Mountain area near the Willamette River, where more and more people are drawing down the aquifer and static water levels are dropping every year, no one we know of is taking increasing amounts of water out of our part of the drainage.

Oddly enough, we are right next door to more than one "city" water system. The neighbor downhill from us has a water line connecting to a water system about two miles on the other side of us and over a ridge. Her water pipe runs along the front of our property. Another neighbor on a large farm also has access to this water system, the Cove Orchard water district, which was established with support from federal money five or six years before we moved into the area when it was discovered that the settlement of Cove Orchard, after draining its septic systems into that little valley for as long as anyone had lived there, had coliform bacteria in its wells.

The neighbor downhill tells us that when she got the chance to hook up, even though she wasn't in the Cove Orchard Valley, she didn't think twice. Desperate for a dependable water supply, she withdrew her entire retirement account and spent it on connecting. To do so, she had to beg and cajole an easement over about two miles of other people's farms and pay for a private contractor to install the pipe. But even though the pipe runs along all 1,500 feet of our frontage, it isn't available to us. It's a two-inch pipe contracted for only one household, and anyway, the members of the water district are chary of their supply and won't vote to let anyone new onto it. Besides that, our neighbor is responsible for repair and upkeep of her pipe all the way to the source. If somebody on one of those farms puts down a post hole in the wrong place and pokes a hole in her pipe, it's up to her to find and repair it, all the while paying the water bill on the leakage.

When workers were putting an international fiber optic cable six feet under our road a few years back, that very thing happened and the neighbor ended up with one big water bill. What fiber optic cable is doing on our road is something else. I've heard that it connects the stock market in Tokyo with the one in New York so financiers can exchange stock information instantaneously. It's strictly a financial enterprise and doesn't do us any immediate good that I know of. This sometimes seems very odd to me, as I look down our gravel country road. Until recently we had a phone service that was so local we couldn't even call our phone company except long distance, and here was this cable six inches from our rural mailbox sending virtually instantaneous financial news about Nike and Mitsubishi between New York and Tokyo.

There's a second water district just about a quarter of a mile across the fields on the other side of the road, this one buying water from the village of Yamhill. Yamhill, about two miles away, is "our town." Yamhill used to pipe its water from a small drainage in the nearby Coast Range, a supply that inevitably would be vulnerable to logging from the thousands of lumber company acres above it, should the timber company that owns it decide one day to take down those big evergreens. Now, however, Yamhill has a municipal well. The secondary water district across the way is a small, independent organization, contracting to buy water from the larger, though still small, Yamhill city water district. The members of this small water district put in their own pipes, vote their own board, pay for their own repairs, and monitor their own water use. It's a water district consisting of about a dozen households and they don't want to deal with any more. And, yes, again, even if we wanted to pay for a pipe across the field and could get an easement to lay it, they wouldn't let us hook up. These country water districts are close-handed with their supply, like medieval fiefdoms. Once you connect, the water isn't cheap and you have a cooperative responsibility to maintain the system. So even if we could cough up the ten or twenty thousand to hook into one of these water districts, they wouldn't let us.

The guy at the mushroom plant on the other end of Lilac Hill Road has been working on ideas for another water district that might include us because he has to truck in thousands of gallons of water every month just to run his plant, but even if he were to swing that and we could get into it, it wouldn't be cheap.

With all this in mind, and considering we were well-rich and water-poor, we tried to figure out what we could do with the system we had. We consulted with the original drillers, who checked our pump equipment, made some minor adjustments, and said there wasn't anything they could do aside from trying for a seventh well on the property. When I asked about the discrepancy between the original water well report and the performance, the well man referred to what he called "the charge."

"Must of used up the charge," he bellowed. The way he said it I knew he didn't mean the forty-dollar bill for coming out to give advice, but I had to ask.

"What charge?"

The well man has an odd manner of speaking. For one thing, he shouts when he talks. I guess that means he's hard of hearing. I can imagine that years of working with the pounding noise of a drill might lead to hearing loss. Besides being loud, his voice also has a strange resonance as if it comes from some deep place in his throat. But it is not the sound of his voice that I find especially odd. It is more the way in which he answers my questions as I try to find out what we ought to do, if there is anything we can do, to improve our water supply.

When I ask him a question, he doesn't look at me and he doesn't answer right away. Instead, his mouth opens, his eyes roll upward, and he seems to be scanning the sky through the oak branches, as if to discover where that querulous female voice is coming from. Then he turns to my husband, not me, and answers as if I weren't there. As if I had not spoken at all.

Loudly he says, "She don't keep up. The charge."

After a few more questions, also answered in this strange indirect way, I decide, for one thing, that he isn't comfortable talking well business with women, at least this woman, and for another, that the charge is the first outpouring of water in a new well. Water stored in reserve in the porous level of soil drains off. After this charge is used up, it's a matter of going with the deep flow. In this case, at first the well probably did, in fact, give seven gallons a minute, but after ten years, maybe even in the first year, the *charge* had been used up and now the well was pumping only half a gallon a minute, maybe less. There was never a time it ran completely out of water, but once we had used up the short reserve of water standing in the well, it was half a gallon per minute or less.

Think about how quickly you fill your bathtub, about how long it takes your toilet to refill after a three-gallon flush, about water left running as you peel potatoes or brush your teeth. Half a gallon per minute is less than you might think. And there had to be a certain amount of water in the well in order for the pump to work. If we drew it down, at half a gallon per minute it would take, for example, half an hour to build up fifteen gallons—enough maybe for a bath, or a load of washing, or five minutes of watering the garden, or a few flushes of the toilet. You don't realize how much water runs through the average household until you start measuring it in half gallons per minute.

Even at half a gallon per minute it seems you might manage to get by. You think that's 720 gallons per twenty-four hour day? Think again. It's not only the overall use—it's a matter of using it evenly. Our well doesn't refill very quickly once it is drawn down. Water use isn't distributed evenly over a twenty-four hour period. When the well is full, water doesn't run in. When it's empty, water runs in slowly.

There we were, with twenty acres, and a garden seemed out of the question. For a rainy state, western Oregon has a surprisingly long summer drought, the heat of which is part of what makes the Willamette Valley one of the world's leading nursery plant producers. And we couldn't even keep a plot of lettuce going. It was a big disappointment. And the daily problems of coordinating water use were depressingly common. We found ourselves running to the pumphouse to reset the switch several times a day, not always with success. We used dishwater to water the flowers growing in pots on the porch. We let the small green tomatoes dry on the vines. Our beautiful farm began to look like a folly. Without a good water supply, land isn't worth much. We also worried that the supply actually might be declining. What if we ended up not with half a gallon of water per minute, but no water at all? We began to look for water alternatives.

When we moved to the place, we had found an old cistern in the front yard. It turned out that this was one of the six "wells" on the place. The other five were drilled wells, but this was a deep reservoir filled during the rainy months by rainwater running off the roof of the house and through a buried pipe that carried water away from the gutters and through an opening in the cement casing of the cistern, about three feet below the ground's surface. The cistern was a cylindrical, concrete-lined hole about five feet across, covered with a rotting piece of plywood. We took the cover off and peered into a darkly reflecting pool of slightly rank-smelling water. Our apprehensive yet hopeful faces were reflected in the subterranean pool. We dropped a weighted rope into the water. One foot, five feet, ten feet, twenty—the rope ran out before we reached bottom. It was deep. And there were no handholds for climbing out if one were to fall in. When the water was down several feet below the lip, as it was when we first pushed aside the rotten plywood, there would be no really good way to climb out should one fall in. It was a mother's nightmare. I shuddered, thinking of the flimsy cover and the two small children of the family who had lived in the house before we bought it.

In some ways the cistern looked like an major accident waiting to happen, a murky pit designed by Edgar Allen Poe. We thought of calling a gravel company to fill it in. But it also looked like gold, considering our water shortage. We decided to try to pump from it, for some minimal gardening at least. To start with, Bill put a two-inch-thick wooden cover over the whole thing, a cover so heavy I could hardly lift the edge, so a child should not be able to budge it.

I remembered once seeing an inexpensive red pitcher pump in an old hardware store. We began to look for a hand pump, but without success. Then one day in the local Sears mail order office, while checking on something else, we noticed a farm catalogue and— what do you know—Sears actually stocked a red pitcher pump of the sort I'd seen. A pitcher pump is limited in how deep it can draw; twenty feet down is the limit. This has to do with hydraulics and air pressure and how far you can sustain a vacuum. But twenty feet would do for our little experiment.

We got the pump. Bill engineered a pipe through the lid of the well and mounted the pump on it. We took turns working the handle and with great delight found that it worked. Rank but clear water gushed into the watering can. This was when we still had all the geese. They were delighted. They came bustling up and had a swim in their Smurf wading pool, which we had adopted as a temporary reservoir for the cistern water. All that summer we used cistern water to sprinkle the flowers in pots around the porch and the hopeful (though not exactly flourishing) small planting of lettuce and tomatoes. As the drought summer turned into fall, the rains failed to return and the water level of the cistern dropped below the capacity of a hand pump to lift it to the surface. But by that time we had enjoyed more than two months of wet benefits, the flowers were beginning to fade anyway, and we were sure it must rain sooner or later. And it did, but not until late December.

The hand pump in the cistern was an adventure and a modest improvement to our water situation. As it was rainwater, we expected it was fairly pure to start with, but of course it often had a stagnant odor after weeks of sitting in the deep dark tank. My father had told me that in Kansas when he was growing up on a farm, rainwater in a cistern was used for the main house supply, but this required annual maintenance. Once a year, he said, the deep cistern was pumped dry and someone descended into it to scrub it clean and coat the interior with a fresh layer of hot paraffin. Then it was ready for refilling. Water kept in the deep, clean vault stayed cool and sweet. Stories like this make me reflect and wonder how many once essential tasks we no longer know how to accomplish. I could not even imagine how to purify our cistern and coat it with hot paraffin. The very idea of descending into that deep cylinder was alarming, as was the idea of dealing with buckets of scalding wax. I think he said that the cistern was filled with rainwater, but there is also some ghost of a memory of water carted from a nearby river. I don't know whether that comes from my father's stories or from somewhere else. It all sounds like a great deal of work compared to turning on a city faucet, but now that we had been brought up short on the difficulties of supplying one of life's essential elements I realized the knowledge, engineering, and sheer hard work that must go into supplying a city—a village, even—with water.

Our cistern made an improvement in that summer's tomatoes and the lettuce patch, but house water still was in short supply. Guests in late summer might find themselves in the middle of a shower without a trickle of water to rinse the suds from their hair. At Thanksgiving we invited sixteen relatives for dinner. We made it through most of the day, but when it was time to wash dishes the water stopped suddenly. The toilet no longer flushed. Guests drank beer or lemonade. The dishes sat until next morning.

It's hard to convey the emotional effect of not having a reliable water system. There are worse things, certainly, but there is something so impoverished and deprived feeling about the way one's household suddenly comes to a stop in most of the basic functioning we associate with civilized life. Toilets, showers, clean clothing, washed vegetables, clean dishes, mopped floors, clean hands. And then there are the amenities, blooming flowers and crisp vegetables, a hose to wash the car or clean off the front sidewalk. Finally there are the economic implications. You have paid a great deal of money for a piece of real estate whose value, without a water supply, may drop to less than you still owe on it. There are places on the eastern side of the Cascades where insufficient water forces residents to buy water and bring it in by truck, but I hadn't counted on living like that.

One of our consultants at the farm store who also runs a pump and irrigation business suggested that one way of dealing with a slow water flow was to put in a reservoir, that is, a large plastic tank with a system of dual pumps and pressure switches. The system would pump regularly on a timed schedule, filling the reservoir tank even when water was not being drawn, then water for the house would be drawn from the reservoir by pressure from a second pump. This system did not actually add water to the system so much as evening out the draw. By regularly drawing down the well itself and taking water into the reservoir, the system allowed more water from the surrounding earth to flow into the well.

It would put more water at our disposal by letting us take more at certain times, and by evening out usage it would prevent the multiple shut-offs we experienced when the well was drawn down.

The system would a cost about twenty-six hundred dollars, with a 1,000-gallon reservoir tank, a second water pump inside the tank, the system of electrical switches and timing devices, the plumbing between the deep well and the reservoir, and the work involved. It sounded like a bargain.

The risk involved was mainly this: by trying to take more water, we might run out entirely, in which case the system simply would pump the final dregs and we'd have spent twenty-six hundred dollars for nothing. But I recently had received a writing check for about that amount. Money in hand, it seemed a chance worth taking.

I love the moment when workmen arrive to begin a certain specialized job, especially if the workmen know what they're doing and have all kinds of extraordinary machinery to make it happen quickly. A backhoe dug out the hole in which the reservoir would be buried. The 1,000-gallon plastic tank was lowered into place. A pump electrician did the wiring between the deep well and the tank, installing a switch box inside our pump house and hooking up the secondary pump in the reservoir. The lid of the reservoir was attached temporarily until it could fill, and the operation was inspected and certified to be in working order. Then the lid was cemented down and bolted in place, and the backhoe moved dirt back over the reservoir.

We stared at the slight mound of dirt over the underground system. It all seemed quite final. I had imagined some sort of tank with a removable lid I could peer into to check the workings and the water level. The reservoir, though it was merely three feet below the earth, was as mysterious and invisible as our 220-foot-deep well shaft. We were cautioned to let it fill for a couple of days at least before trying to do anything radical, like wash the dirty laundry. For two days, we took sixty-second showers and used water sparingly in other ways. Our water had a heavy chlorine smell because the last thing the workmen did before sealing it up was to chlorinate the whole system. The chlorine would pass out of the system and evaporate; this was just a procedure to deal with any contamination that might have occurred in the process of installing the system. Gradually the smell disappeared and we began to use our water system in a more normal way. Weeks passed, then months. Once the system ran out of water when a valve hooked up to the sheep's watering trough broke and our entire water supply drained out into the pasture. Another time we had six house guests for two weeks and on the last day of their visit the well went dry, briefly—which meant that the system had been unable to keep up with two weeks worth of extra showers and laundry. We still couldn't let a sprinkler run unattended in the garden, but we could do some small-time watering, water the animals, and carry on in the house more or less like anyone else.

The lack of water for a large country garden was still a problem, however. This whole process of trying to solve our water problems had been stretched out over a matter of four years. During all that time we had been mulching a garden spot with hay and manure from the barn, and what had been baked clay soil had become looser and richer. Some of our gardening efforts worked out, such as garlic planted the fall before which could benefit from the winter rains, develop heads in spring, ripen and dry out for harvest in July. In other cases we used cold frames to start lettuce early, when there still were spring rains and when a glassed-in frame would create its own misty climate under a soft early sun. But without water, corn dried on the stalk; tomatoes grew into pulpy, undersized red balls, barely edible; and carrots and other root vegetables became impacted in the baked earth as the Willamette Valley summer drought burned on.

The cistern was still working in its third summer of restoration. The Coyote reservoir system was doing beautifully in its second year, within its natural limitations. That accounted for two of the six wells on the place. We inspected the other four. One was at the bottom of the west pasture. It consisted of a four-inch-diameter pipe in the ground with no cover. We could see water close to the surface. When we dropped a weighted cable down it, we found that it was probably at least 150 feet deep. The disadvantage was that there was no pumping equipment in place, nor was there an electric line to it. Another well existed at the top of the same pasture but it had been welded shut with a heavy metal cover. Presumably it held water but it would have been difficult to check, and it too was lacking in pipe, pump, pump house, and electricity. Another well was only about twenty feet from the house, presumably the first of the various wells and the oldest. Like all the others, it contained water and seemed to be anywhere from 150 to 200 feet deep. It was in a small pumphouse but all equipment for hooking it up had been removed here too.

The final pump was in the walnut grove between the house and Lilac Hill Road. It had an electrical wire running to the pumphouse that enclosed it, a water tank, and a submersible pump deep within, with all the usual electric circuit breakers and wiring, but it wouldn't work. This seemed to have been the most recent well prior to the one hooked up to the house. We called the pump man once again and asked him to come look at it. He told us that if the wiring to the pumphouse was good and if most of the pipe in the well was good, it would cost about eight hundred dollars to put the whole system back on line. There was no telling what that would do to our other, main water supply. The two wells were far apart, on opposite sides of the property, and there probably would be no noticeable drawdown of one by the other, but you could never tell what was going on down there at 220 feet. Moreover, this older well seemed to have water now, but it might not last. It had been sitting unused for at least twelve years and no doubt had developed a "charge" that would be drawn off when it went back into use. It was unlikely that the well would provide a heavy flow of water. It probably was in the half-gallon-per-minute bracket too, since it had been abandoned for the newest well—obviously one more failed attempt at getting a decent water supply

We told the pump man to go ahead with the project, asking him to put a low-capacity pump on this well, one that would pump no more than four gallons per minute. Our aim was to have a garden well, not a supplement for the house supply, which was doing all right with the Coyote system and reservoir. With a low-capacity pump, perhaps there would be less tendency to pump it down too quickly.

The workman who installed the new pump in the old well was young and handsome—he looked a bit like Martin Sheen at the *Apocalypse Now* age. He took a lot of breaks to smoke out there in the walnut grove, cupping his hands to shield the wooden match and jutting his chin out, the cigarette balanced between his lips, then holding his cigarette between thumb and forefinger the way one holds a dart. The grass was dry, the breeze was hot. I watched him surreptitiously and thought about summer grass fires and lung cancer, but I just wanted him to get the job done so I didn't say anything. He had an even younger helper, the boss's son I'd guess, whom he directed to hold, lift, and carry the various implements required to put the well back in use. To begin with, they had to pull up the old pump and the two hundred feet of pipe upon which it was suspended. The pipe came up in twenty-foot lengths, spilling buckets of cold water around the demolished pumphouse, and each length had to be unscrewed, then laid to one side for reuse. The electric wire attached to the pump came along with it, and this he dropped in loose coils to the side of the pipe. The pipe looked relatively clean, a good sign I assumed. Nothing rusty, nothing terribly worn. When he finished hauling up the last pipe, the old pump came out of its pit and I saw how heavy it was, a motor with a filter and metal casing shaped like something NASA might shoot into outer space. The well repairman pronounced the pump unusable, the pipe usable.

Then the process began in reverse: the new pump and the new wire went back into the hole, a twenty-foot length of pipe screwed on at every interval. The workman also added a new switch and circuit breaker at the top and wired it all up. When it was all ready to go and he had set the pump running to clear the water, I took a glass out to the yard and drew off half a pint. It was milky with bubbles, or perhaps there was a whitish sediment in it from the deep clay, but otherwise it looked good and had no particular smell at all. When it began to run clear, I decided to taste it. One concern was that the well had been abandoned because it had turned salty. Below our rolling hills are old sea beds. Wells dug too deeply or in the wrong spot sometimes go salty. We had heard stories of someone down the road who'd spent fifteen thousand dollars to get a new well, only to have it come up salty. I tasted the water in my glass. It tasted like pure, neutral water. No off odors. No salt. No funny taste. I had not known I could feel such joy at the taste of water.

We've been using this new, second well for two years now. Although it's set up so that we can switch it to the house system if we want to, except for one time when the other well needed a minor repair we haven't done so. We have used it for gardening and other outdoor purposes, as well as for reserve in case of emergency. We've been able to water the garden abundantly and regularly, with the delightful result of producing a full range of vegetables and keeping the flowers alive as well. So far it has never failed us. We don't use it during the winter, of course, because anything growing gets the benefit of the winter rains. If this well has used up its "charge," we can't tell—or perhaps leaving it unused during the winter months lets it recharge. And so far as we can tell, there's been no change for the worse in our old well either.

After six years on the place we'd finally arrived at a regular, usable water supply for all our purposes. Still, we don't take it for granted, nor do we waste water. We don't have a lot of water, just barely enough. We've installed a new, water-conserving toilet and a low-water-use shower head, and we use reduction screens on the water faucets in the kitchen and bathroom. We continue to mulch the garden and flower beds, and have switched to watering with a soaker hose and drip irrigation instead of a sprinkler.

The two wells seem to serve our needs, but we still pump some water out of the old cistern when we water the boxed plants along the porch and those near the house. A small grey-green frog with golden eyes lives within the red pump, and when we start, slowly, to work the handle, he crawls out on the lip and hides there under the spout until we've finished. He, too, enjoys the cistern. We treat him with respectful care, as befits a resident water spirit.

Going to the Source

One of the pleasures of country life is going on buying trips. These are not like city shopping trips, all escalators and fitting rooms, shoe salesmen and displays of food processors, perfume sampled on the braceleted wrist, and lunch in some pleasant little place with vegetarian burritos, mineral water, and sixteen kinds of muffins. Nor are they like suburban forays, dedicated driving trips from mall to mall to find a microwave oven or children's school clothes. Country shopping trips frequently take you through pleasant scenery over roads you have never driven before, roads with names like Walnut Hill and Old Church, Mossy Creek and Gopher Valley. They introduce you to people whose lives are intriguing and practical, who can give you the benefit of experience and teach you a lesson or two. Whether you are off to get a yellow daylily named "Butterfly Owl" or to get a pickup load of cow manure, country shopping trips take you right to the source.

Our trip to buy a ram lamb was like that. The woman who had the lamb also raised llamas. Her house was decorated with tapestry weave blankets in a traditional southwestern style made by her father-in-law. She was an attractive woman, tall, slender, in a cowboy shirt, jeans, and wooden clogs. She and her husband were in the process of installing a New Zealand electric fence since a dog attack had devastated her daughter's flock of 4-H Romneys the month before. Many of the ewes still showed signs of scarring, where the wool had not yet grown back over the wounds. Chris, the woman, was still troubled about the dog attack, but she also was optimistic and it was clear she loved and cared for her animals. I thought she looked as if she could have been a model. I wondered who did the heavy work around the place until, with one long, slender arm she scooped up the hefty ram lamb of our choice, flopped him gently on his rump, and gave him a scheduled injection before we took him home.

On another trip, to buy a colony of bees, my daughter and I met the beekeeper. The beekeeper had been in the hospital with pneumonia. He was home now but still feeling weak, so his son would be going out to the fields to help us load our bees. It was early spring and the weather was fitful, chilly and wet one minute, windy and bright the next, and to keep the beekeeper comfortable, a big old iron stove had been stoked to a high heat in the middle of the house. To keep out drafts, the windows and doors had been hung with blankets, so the inside of the house was dimly lit by artificial lights and full of furry, drowsy heat. Besides chairs and tables, an old couch, and a recliner where the beekeeper sat before the stove reading westerns, the house was full of bee equipment, stacks of empty comb, hivebodies stored till the main honeyflow, and containers of honey, so that the whole house smelled of honey and comb, the fertile pollen-permeated smell of bees. In all of this dim buzzing heat, this smell of hive and flower, the beekeeper sat, a peaceful, frail-looking elderly gentleman with a soft, curious voice. He had large, dark eyes and his eyebrows curled long and tendril like.

He told us about his life in beekeeping. During the summers he had a permit from the Forest Service to transport his hives into the high Cascades, where the bees could harvest nectar from mountain meadows of wildflowers. "They're interesting little critters," he said. "I wish I was starting all over." My daughter and I looked at one another and registered the same thought: the dark-eyed, frail beekeeper in his heated honey-scented hive had become a sort of human honey bee.

Going to buy the two border collies when we first moved to the farm three years ago was also an adventure. Jack, a large, smooth-coated dog, came from a farm on the east side of the Willamette Valley. As we parked and got out of the car, we heard loud voices around the corner of the barn. We hesitated, but then a sturdy red-faced woman and a big boy of twelve or so who looked just like her came around the corner hauling an oversized sack of feed. She clearly was carrying most of the weight, and was letting him hear about it. "We've come about the dog," I said.

Eventually we transacted our business. The dog breeder, who turned out to be a pleasant, forthright woman, and extremely able with her dogs, showed us the pups, as well as the abilities of her working dogs. The father of the pups was an enthusiastic smooth collie, black and white, imported from Wales the year before. He was a super jumper, flying over the highest fences, and when the flock started the wrong way he ran across their backs and turned them. We were so impressed by this high-energy, good-looking dog that we picked the pup that looked most like him.

Our second border collie came from a different breeder, not a sheep dog trials person but an older woman who'd worked her dogs in obedience for years, and this expedition, too, took us on an interesting trip. She lived on the top of a mountain on the way to the coast. There she had seven or eight dogs penned around the yard. They were "rough," that is, long-haired border collies, on the small side, elegant and wasp-waisted, with luxuriant plumy coats. Before picking out the pup we named Mollie, I spent two or three hours visiting with the woman and looking through forty years worth of scrapbooks on all the dogs she'd ever had and trained. She'd moved to the mountain, she said, so that she could have her dogs without bothering anyone. The farm was wild and beautiful, with acres of old oak trees and a broad, sunny upland pasture in the middle, a virtual kingdom of dogs. Her home was a casual, open sort of place developed around a trailer. From the chairs in the yard I got the feeling that she lived out-of-doors as much as in. In the front room of the house was a dog bed and a dark-eyed, broad-headed older border collie giving me a warning eye.

"Don't get too close," said the old woman, "but come here. I want to show you something."

She reached into the dog's bed and came up with a fat hairless pup about the size of a hamster. The pup looked like a tiny pig.

"They're Chihuahuas. Their mother couldn't feed them so the owner brought them to me. Tar here was just weaning her own pups. She liked them okay, but these, they're her prizes. Watch out you don't reach for one, she'll bite."

Later we picked out Mollie. She was a black border collie with a gray-spotted white muzzle and feet. My nephew, Nick, had come along on the trip, and eight-week-old Mollie fell asleep on his lap in the car on the way home.

These have been some of my favorite country shopping trips, but there have been many more, including the trip to buy alfalfa from the broad-faced farmer who stood first on one leg, then the other, as he plucked at the skin on his neck and talked about the weather; the trip to buy daylilies from a home nursery where a delightful woman showed us an arbor decked with sixteen-year-old kiwi vines the thickness of a working man's arm, and a back yard full of her husband's bonsai collection; the trip to buy sheep at a farm in the hills where you had to wash your boots in chlorinated water before you went through the gate, the collies and Abyssinian cats had their own house complete with bathing facilities, and all the barns had classical music playing in them; and the trip to a Columbia River farm where we ended up not buying anything but got the benefit of a long lesson in colored sheep genetics by the enthusiastic woman who lived there.

Of course sometimes the trips aren't so profitable. The other day we followed a series of hand-lettered signs in red paint offering gooseberry bushes for sale, only to encounter a woman with brightly dyed maroon hair piled into a remarkably tall "beehive" hairdo, peering suspiciously at us through her screen door. When I expressed interest in buying some gooseberry bushes, she muttered, "Don't have any. We had one but it looked dead so we stuck it back in the ground."

Of course, most of our time is spent not shopping at all. In fact, another side of life in the country has to do with the pleasures of *not* buying—not buying apples or cherries because our trees are laden; not buying lettuce because ours is so tender, abundant, and fresh; not buying eggs because our hens are generous; not even buying a ticket to the movies in town as often as we used to because the sunsets from our front porch are so gorgeous. But *not* buying things, that's a different story.

Equinox

The day my father died, my youngest sister called. Her sad voice on the phone said, "Daddy passed away this morning." We had known he could not live much longer. I'd last seen him the week before when my oldest daughter and I had gone to visit. "Remember your old granddad," he said to Monica with a smile, and they embraced. We left him sitting in the yard, looking out into the trees where the humming birds and finches clustered at his feeders and darted up into the tall firs and cedars that circle the place. By the next week, the cancer had spread and he could no longer eat, but I thought I would have time for one more visit and was planning to drive to Coos Bay at the end of the week. After my sister called, the words "passed away" haunted my thoughts for their connotations of journey and location. Where was my father, now? It took me about four hours to drive to Coos Bay—four hours during which I had time to consider the reality of death and try to accustom myself to the beginning of my father's long absence. Sometimes the tears ran down my face, and other times I merely studied traffic and landscape and made my way south.

My sisters and mother and I made arrangements with the funeral director. Father had asked to be cremated. When the question of what to do with his ashes came up, Mother said he had wanted them to be carried out to sea by his friends at the tugboat company for which he had taken so many pictures, and there, on the way to Hawaii, scattered on the waves.

I found myself interrupting. "May I have some?" My mother and sisters looked at me in surprise. "Just a little bit," I added lamely.

Mother thought a moment and said, well, sure, that would be okay, since he had liked the farm a lot and enjoyed spending time there. We visited his body and each of us touched his hair and left a departing kiss. As we left the room where his body lay, wearing a finely striped cotton shirt, his curly gray hair so neatly combed, his eyes closed, his familiar hands folded on the tucked sheet pulled up under his arms, I found myself saying aloud, "'Bye Daddy," as I had often done when leaving a room where he sat or the porch where he stood to wave us off after a visit. It gave me a sense of familiarity and contact. The director said we could pick up the ashes the day of the memorial.

The service at St. Monica's Catholic church was gratifyingly well attended. Members of the family and others stood up to reminisce about my father. People talked about his flying, his little red Piper J3, his picture taking, his creative spirit and inspiration, his good and friendly acts over the years. His favorite camera and a black-and-white photo of him with his airplane sat next to a vase of flowers on a small table at the front of the church. It was comforting and pleasant to look at these concrete signs of his interesting and devoted character. He was a father to be proud of, one who had given us sustenance, love, and creative encouragement throughout all our lives.

Back at the house, my two sisters, my brother, and I all took out our cameras—as did a number of Father's photo friends—and began taking pictures of the many family friends and relatives who filled the house and garden. The day was well recorded on film. At one point, someone took a picture of Jane, Richard, Suzy, and me all lined up and looking through the lenses of our various cameras. We called it a "four-camera salute" to our photographer dad.

Later, according to directions, I went to the mortuary to pick up "my" box of ashes. I was a little nervous, wondering whether I had done the wrong thing out of some primitive, possessive impulse that said I was not ready to let go of the last of my father's mortal remains. Later, the captain of the tugboat who took the rest of the ashes to sea sent my mother a copy of the ship's log for the day on which the ashes were scattered. It was reported to be "calm, beautiful..." and the record gave the latitude and longitude of the event, halfway to Hawaii—a place where my parents had spent at least one winter month a year for the past several years.

So here I had this errant bit of my father's ashes, "my share," and I wondered whether I was being selfish or superstitious, and also, whether he would have objected to having his ashes thus divided. I was comforted by the fact that he had been an indulgent father, never one to turn down an offspring's request if at all possible. The box was heavier than I had expected, and inside was a plastic bag sealed with a twisty-tie, like something on a bread wrapper. When I was alone at home, I opened the bag to see what the contents were like and to ponder on what, exactly, I wanted to do with them.

It is a painful thing to lose one's loved father, even if he is 78 and, practically speaking, one is well-raised and independent and has raised children of one's own. My thoughts were mainly that he was no longer suffering the suffocating pain of the disease, and that certainly in his place I would not have wanted to prolong dying beyond that point. But they also were hovering around a certain empty spot in my imagination, that spot to which many of the events of my life had been directed. Specifically, I wanted to tell my father what I was doing.

I wanted to tell him interesting things that came to mind, what I had accomplished, or what I was hoping to do. I will never, I think, get over wanting to tell him about some remarkable event, some bird sighting or journey, some boat trip or plane flight or vision of a Cascade mountain meadow or Mediterranean sunrise. Recently I spotted a lazuli bunting, at our garden bird bath, an uncommon sighting, and when the sun flashed turquoise from its throat, I thought, I want to tell Dad about it. Missing someone is very much involved with wanting to share life's experiences with that person. Social interaction in my family, and I assume in most other families, involves a lot of exchanging of stories, and thus we enlarge upon life and our mutual enjoyment of it.

My father's ashes were coarse and pleasantly colored, pink and white heavy grit, dry crumbles of bone that resembled the coarse sand one finds on certain cove beaches along the Oregon coast, such as the small beach below the gardens at Shore Acres park, where the shells of millions of tiny creatures mix with the sparkling grains of ground quartz, jasper, and other stone, to make a fascinating sand that is not quite yet sand, but still, on a very small scale, retains the form and texture of its previous state. I have taken close-up and micro pictures of that sand, and the tendency is to want to look smaller and smaller and yet smaller, to see how small a bit of matter can be before it loses its individuality. My pictures of the Shore Acres beach show diversity in the smallest scale. So, too, my father's ashes seemed very individual, warmly colored and robust, like his once-reddish brown, curly Scotsman's hair and ruddy complexion. I recognized his long-boned, cheerful angularity in its minuscule, granular form.

Unsure of what I wanted to do with the ashes, I put them in my bedroom cupboard for a while, trusting that the next step would become obvious sooner or later. This was at the end of July, and I really did not want to give up my father. I thought of the many times during my life when my father helped me through some minor crisis or simply was good company, as he always was. When I had been ill for several months as a seven-year-old, he took me to work with him during my recovery, in order to get me out in the fresh air and to strengthen my muscles weakened by weeks of lying in bed. He worked for the telephone company back then. We would drive in the telephone truck to the country around Clatskanie and Vernonia in the wilds of northwestern Oregon, not far from the farm where we live now, "looking for trouble," as the telephone business called it. I loved to go looking for trouble with my dad. He would go into the brush with his heavy belt of tools around his waist and his climbing hooks on, and climb poles, testing wires and connections, fiddling with insulators, making changes or repairing breaks, while I wandered around below finding pretty rocks, enjoying the dappled light, and stirring up quail or deer in the underbrush.

For some reason, I often think of him taking me to college in the old Buick, which blew its engine on the return trip and never ran again, and the night he drove for two hours through a storm to pick up my husband and me when our own car failed on that same road in 1964. When each of the three children was born, I loved bringing them home to present to the grandparents. Father was the one to take the first photos, always wonderful portraits, sure to show the babies in their most beautiful and liveliest light.

He was interested when we bought a farm a few years back and moved out of the city, especially when we decided to raise sheep. He had a lot of stories about sheep from the old days back in Kansas, when he was growing up and when he and my mother were first married and lived on the family farm. It was my father who had conceived the idea of moving west from Kansas. He had traveled to Oregon with friends and fallen in love with the mountains and coast of Oregon. When he and my mother married, he promised to take her out West. And west they went, when I was two, in 1941. A love of beautiful landscape marked his whole life. He regularly took us for long and short trips into the most beautiful spots the Northwest could offer and passed along his love of nature and all its sensory delights.

Fall came and the box of ashes remained in my cupboard. I remembered how closely my photographer-pilot father followed the seasons of light and shadow. On the longest day of the year he could hardly contain his pleasure and sense of celebration. At the spring and fall equinox he never failed to mention the change of light and the direction of the season. In winter, as days grew shorter and shorter, he commented on the lengthening dark, lest anyone not notice it, and conveyed a slight feeling of apprehension as if, were we not attentive enough, we might forget to turn and start the movement back to light. On the first day after the winter solstice, there was relief in his voice and soon he would comment on the fact that he already could tell that it was getting lighter, and how pleased that made him.

One day I awoke and realized that though the sun blazed hot and pleasant on the oak canopy at the top of the farm, and on the open grassland around it, we had reached the autumnal equinox. Thereafter the days would be shorter than the nights. Having learned this lesson from childhood at my father's knee, something told me it was time to let go of my father, at least as much as I could. I took the box from my cupboard and went to the edge of the oak grove where, with the shadows of the trees at my back, I could look out over the valley and see gold upon gold of harvest fields and the blue shadow of the Coast Range beyond. I thought about calling my sisters, but decided against it. I didn't want to usurp some privilege, but I also didn't want to engineer someone else's idea of leave-taking from our father, nor was I sure that they wouldn't consider my involvement with his mortal remains morbid.

I opened the box and undid the bag within. I took some of the ashes and scattered them around the oak grove, casting them up to the branches and letting them fall where they would. When I had scattered half the ashes, I went into the house and opened the kitchen cupboard. I rarely drink hard liquor, preferring wine or beer, but my father often liked a shot of whisky as an evening "snort" as he called it. When he came to visit, he sometimes brought a bottle in case my cupboard was bare, and I had the remains of the last bottle of whisky he'd brought on his last visit. I poured myself a "snort." I went back to the oak grove and sat on a stump facing southwest. I sipped my whisky, silently toasting my dad and remembering how he loved flying as I watched the redtail hawks circle far out in the valley.

The first time he had gone up in an airplane, oddly, was the day of the stock market crash in 1929. He was fifteen and had persuaded a neighboring barnstormer to take him up. After that he couldn't stay away from planes, though his mother was afraid for him and his dad didn't encourage it. With his brother and other neighborhood kids he played around the neighbor's airplane, sometimes even flying it from one end of the wheat field to the other. He told me they would fly it close to the ground and land, then get out, lift up the tail and turn it around, and fly it back the other way. My father's childhood seemed wonderfully privileged in some ways. They were farmers and never particularly well off materially, but he had a horse named Gypsy and could ride with his friends all over the county, meeting on winter days at some snowy crossroads to race their horses and have a day of talk and games. It seemed wonderful enough to have your own horse to roam about the countryside, but the idea that he actually had been able to go out and fly on such a casual basis dumbfounded me.

I felt better after I had scattered half the ashes on this day of the autumnal equinox. The shot of whisky was pleasant, too. I let the feeling drift down my throat and through my limbs, and the burning taste of the alcohol imparted a pleasant, ritualistic feeling. I still was not ready to part with him completely, however. So I left half the ashes in the bag and returned the box to my cupboard. "Sorry, Daddy," I said to the sunshine. "It's hard to let go."

The months went by, and one spring day I realized that my internal alarm had gone off and was letting me know it was the spring equinox, another beautiful day that would have been wonderful for flying—bright and sunny, with very little wind. I could see for miles down the valley, all the way to where the shadow of Marys Peak, forty miles away, humped up in the Coast Range outside Corvallis. I missed my father very much and expected I always would. But it was time. I took the box from my cupboard. On this day I went to the vineyard, on the other side of the property, to the east. I took the rest of the ashes, handful by handful, and tossed them into the air over the vineyards. They caught the sun and floated in a shining cloud. Some of them came down, but some of them whirled up in a current of warm air and moved aloft.

Bill was in the vineyard checking the vitality of the vines after winter. It looked like an early year. When I had scattered the last of the ashes, he went to the wineroom and siphoned off two glasses of last year's pinot noir, not yet bottled. We sat in the shade of trees at the top of the vineyard and drank a toast to my father.

Time has passed. We still live on the farm. There's always something to do, something to look at. When we first moved here, there didn't seem to be so many birds around, but every year the number has grown. I don't know what that means except, perhaps, the environment has improved for birds because we've resisted spraying unless we felt we had no choice. We've also mulched the garden and other areas, and we keep water and feeders out. Barn swallows have moved into the new barn, and each year their numbers increase so now, on summer days, dozens of them sail above the pasture catching insects. One year, Bill raised a batch of gourds. He dried them and cut small, round, bird doors in some, hanging them on poles along the driveway. Greenbacked swallows moved in. We've had increasing visits from bluebirds, too, especially in late winter when they come to clean off the mistletoe berries and dive down into the flower garden out front for a dip at the bird bath. And there was that lazuli bunting. And the grosbeaks. And a Bullock's oriole. And two pileated woodpeckers that showed up in the spring. We have a lot of hawks around. The redtails seem to come back every year to nest in the woods above the west pasture and spend a lot of time circling on air currents over the place, whole families of them it appears, spiraling up and up and calling their thrilling cries. There are also kestrels on the wires along the road, and some mallards in the little pond at the bottom of the pasture, and both rough-legged and marsh hawks.

Recently we've had a new sighting. During the past year a smaller hawk appeared in the upper oak grove. We've tried to identify it but are not sure what it is. It has beautiful large eyes and a long narrow tail and seems to be a bird hunter. It flies with a swift, perilous motion that sends the smaller birds up and away before it. Recently we realized there were two of them, and now it seems there might be a young one, because after we thought the others had flown off one morning, a slightly smaller bird flopped down from the branches of the oak onto the roof of the barn and squeaked as if complaining and begging the others to come back. It has given us a good look at its magnificent eyes and dark head, the fluttering loose white feathers with dark markings at the top of its legs, the dark bars on its tail and the lighter ones on its breast.

How interesting and satisfying to have these wonderful birds so close. For several days the adults gave us a show every morning, making their varied calls and flying low over the driveway, landing on the telephone pole, flying up into the trees, then floating down and crossing over the house. I don't know quite what was going on.

In the past few days they seem to have gone elsewhere, but once in a while I hear one and go out to see the distinctive form cross the air above the new barn. It gives me a great deal of pleasure to see them. Sometimes I think about how my father loved to fly more than just about anything, and how he loved birds and the natural world. Then I miss my dad and wish I could tell him about the hawk on the barn roof, and am also suffused with a wonderful joyous feeling that I don't need to.

Wine

Yamhill County, where we live, is full of hills, particularly as river bottom farmland gives way to the foothills of the Oregon Coast Range, which divides the valley from the flats and beaches of the Oregon coast forty miles away. From my front porch I like to look at how the landscape moves: this way, that way, this way, that way, in a series of receding curves until the patchwork of green wheat or golden straw, red plowed dirt and purple-tinged pea vine, blue-green Christmas trees and wild rose-bordered pasture, recedes finally into the blue humps of the Coast Range mountains. Not only is the area full of rolling hills but there are several large ridges—the Amity Hills, Chehalem Ridge, Parrett Mountain—that divide the county into a series of smaller valleys. Rivers that course through them are the Yamhill and the Tualatin, which wind their separate ways until they reach the Willamette River, within the larger Willamette Valley that encompasses all the smaller valleys in a geographical entity.

There are various soils within the county. Our varieties happen to be Willakenzie on the east slope and Hazelaire to the west, both of them variations on "silty clay loam" and both offering variations of percolation, drainage, and slope suitable for growing wine grapes. At deep levels, the soil gives way to rock formations or slippery layers of compressed clay, and below that, the earth's mysteries.

For years I lived somewhere else, but I have long roots here, because when I was two years old and my parents moved from Kansas to Oregon, they lived for a while in Forest Grove, a small town about ten miles north of where we live now. This was at the beginning of World War II, in 1941. Eventually my father was drafted, and then he was sent back home because he was the only telephone man available to service the ammunition dump in that remote area of Oregon near Clatskanie, on the lower Columbia River, not far from the coast. In Forest Grove we lived in a big, white apartment building with a green lawn and a pleasant "victory garden" in a space behind white latticework out back. Our apartment was on the ground floor in front. The back stairway led to the second floor apartment of Mrs. Phillips and her son Andrew. I don't know how old Andrew was—old, I thought, and his mother seemed very old. She reminded me of the picture I'd seen of "Whistler's Mother," with a long, dark dress, and some sort of cap on her head. In memory's imagined rooms, I see Mrs. Phillips sitting in profile, with a white cap and long, dark dress, hands folded in her lap.

Her son, Andrew, was said to be a gold prospector. I don't know whether he had any other sort of job, but from time to time Andrew would leave home for weeks and travel into the hills to look for gold. One time he gave my friend Darrel and me each a black rock and said it had gold in it. The rock didn't look like gold, but I imagined a shiny nugget of purest yellow inside, like something from a Bugs Bunny cartoon I'd seen at the Grove Theater. I sometimes thought of cracking open the rock and claiming the treasure, but I had a sense that this would spoil it somehow, so I simply kept the rock, intact, with my other valuables. Andrew and his mother continued to live in the upstairs apartment as long as we were there, so I guess he never struck it rich, but looking back at Andrew's expeditions more than fifty years later I can see that looking for gold was as good an excuse as any for an extended camping trip into the hills of western Oregon.

Besides bringing back stories of gold, Andrew also told about a spring he'd found in the mountains. He said it glowed at night and gave off a strong odor. Since moving back to this area, I've never heard of such a place, but I've wondered if there might actually have been some sort of mineral spring glowing with phosphorescence. In any case, the rolling landscape continues to make wonderful promises.

The treasure of the hills nowadays is in the vine. During the past twenty years, Yamhill County has become known for its vineyards, from which dozens of vintners produce their distinctive pinot noirs and chardonnays. The area also produces some other varieties such as pinot gris, Müller Thurgau, and Riesling, but excellent pinot noir is what put the area on the world's wine map and brings visitors from all over the world to the annual summer International Pinot Noir Festival on the Linfield College campus in McMinnville. There were vineyards and wineries in Oregon in the early days, but prohibition put them out of business, people forgot about them, and it was not until the 1970s that some visionary winemakers moved to the area and started planting the pinots. In our small vineyard, we have an acre each of pinot noir and chardonnay. When we first moved to Lilac Hill farm, the vines were little more than cuttings, a year or two old, in danger of disappearing forever beneath wild blackberries (which are not native but have taken to the landscape of western Oregon as if they were). Bill did the clearing, ripped out blackberries and scotch broom, and cultivated the ground around the baby vines—for weeks his arms were covered with scratches. In spite of his hard work, we found that many of the original grape plantings did not survive. But the previous owner also had left a bed of rooted cuttings at the top of the vineyard, and from these Bill gradually transplanted vines to fill in the blank spots where the originals died.

Besides the pinots and chardonnays, there also was a small but vigorous planting of another variety that the previous owners had not planted but which they called zinfandel. These so-called zinfandels were mature, thick, woody vines, producing heavy clusters of dark reddish-purple grapes that first October after we moved in, so we made wine from them. The wine was a beautiful deep red, high in sugar and thus high in alcohol, but odd tasting, very tannic with a strong flavor of olive oil. Definitely not zinfandel. Our kids nicknamed it triple-x. Whatever it was, it was ours, so we made it, drank it quite a bit too soon, and waited for the pinots and chardonnays to mature.

Our second fall on Lilac Hill we got enough of the other grapes to make a small batch of pinot and a slightly larger batch of chardonnay. It was a start. The normal yield for an acre of grapes at the height of production would be about two tons, more in some cases. We got about one hundred forty pounds all together, enough for maybe ten gallons of juice. Normally, with good treatment and favorable weather, a new vineyard can produce a fair crop of grapes after a couple of years, but these vines had not been tended properly in their infancy and thus were stunted. With such a hard start, would they be permanently affected? Was it worth the effort to save them? We consoled ourselves with stories of hardship producing fine wines and waited for things to get better.

It's apparently true that stressed vines can produce good wine, due to some peculiarity of minerals in a meager soil, the sun's parching rays that wither the vines and ripen the fruit, or the intensification of flavor resulting from a small crop. Examples of fortuitous stress could be stretched so far as to include the *pourriture noble*—or noble rot   brought on by botrytis, a grayish black mold that somehow produces a wonderful flavor in wine made from the decaying grapes and which is encouraged in France. Another happy disaster courted by German winemakers involves leaving the grapes on the vines until they freeze in late fall, after which they are used to produce "ice wine," which uses the dehydrating effects of freezing to produce a concentrated and flavorful wine. This is all short of actual vine death, of course. We hoped that somehow our vines' struggle to survive would give them a lot of character, which is good in wine, as in people.

Like sheep, wine has a long-held ritual association. From the Bacchanalian cults to the Christian communion, wine has been associated with renewal and vitality. No wonder. Nothing looks so dead as a grape vine in winter. "Bud break"—the moment in spring when, after months of apparent death, the woody corpse of the grapevine again pushes forth the small nubs that will turn into leaves, shoots, and grapes—is always amazing. In tending our grapes, bringing them back from near death, and making our own wine, we hoped we were taking part in something ancient and meaningful.

Moreover, there was romance in the process. Pinot noir grapes are the ones used in France to make Burgundy. Burgundy is a region characterized by smaller vineyards and more quirky products than Bordeaux, where the famous Cabernet Sauvignon grapes are grown to make Bordeaux wines. California is America's version of the Bordeaux area. Oregon is pinot country.

I am, of course, an amateur in describing the compelling flavors of pinot noir and chardonnay. Professional wine critics practice their art by calling up words such as "fresh and spicy, with a strong toasty note to the core of honey-scented citrus flavors, lean and almost racy"; "a bitter edge to the sturdy apple and walnut flavors; "black cherry, currant and anise...with fine touches of spicy oak and silky texture"; and "a solidly built, chunky red." Negative reviews use such language as "earthy, sweaty decadent flavors"; "unappealing cardboardlike flavors"; and even, with not entirely negative intent, "a touch of the barnyard." Because the flavors of wine are complex and infinitely variable, descriptors are a challenge. Good reviews of pinot noir tend to use dark fruit imagery, such as berries or prunes, with spices and tannins, influenced by the stems or skins of the grape, or the barrel used for aging, invoked for character. Chardonnays also are often described for their fruit flavors, particularly in terms of yellow fruits such as grapefruit or lemon, with the additional rounder qualities of the flavor being associated with tastes such as butterscotch or honey. I often have heard that taste depends on smell, and smell is certainly important in wine. A whiff of sulfur from the preservatives used to stop fermentation is deadly to the taste, and the off-smell of oxidized wine from a badly corked bottle is a definite killjoy.

I also have heard that we have only a simple range of tastes—salt, sweet, bitter, sour—and that all tastes are some variety of these four. But in tasting wine this seems impossibly simplified, because the complex tastes and aromas in a good wine seem to resound with endless variety from all parts of the mouth and nose. So, although I might describe any one glass of wine immediately experienced in all its complexity, I can't claim to have a sophisticated enough palette memory to say, exactly, what the taste of our wine is like. Fruity, yes, but not sweet. Wonderful with food of all sorts. Sometimes grapefruit, sometimes currants, sometimes berries. Once in the chardonnay a definite atmosphere of pineapple. In the pinot, what is that flavor? An aroma of raspberries? Tobacco? A hint of pepper? The sharp-sweet taste of an Italian prune? Whatever—it's good. Especially with a grilled lambchop seasoned with homegrown garlic and rosemary; a serving of steamed, small yellow Russian banana potatoes from the garden; a salad of our own fresh greens with olive oil and balsamic vinegar; a wedge of homemade foccaccia seasoned with olive oil and homegrown herbs. Wild apple pie for dessert. Good food—good wine. The key ingredients homegrown. This is luxury.

In those first years, however, we didn't know how the vineyard would turn out. I only knew that the opportunity to produce our own wine took me back to my first encounter with a wine culture, when I lived on the Greek island of Korfu for several months in the early 1960s. In the village where I stayed, we had the local wine each night with our supper omelet, meatballs, or fried sardines. It was a deep purple and tasted wonderful, especially accompanied by a slab of feta and Greek bread or a tomato salad laced with the local olive oil. One afternoon I came out of the hostel to see several of the young women of the village walking along wringing out their purple-stained skirts, laughing and talking among themselves. I was excited to learn they actually had been crushing the grapes with their feet. I was too late to climb into the vat myself, but I went to the barn and there saw the winemaker squeezing the last dregs of juice from a great wooden press. The juice ran down a stained wooden trough into a bucket. Baby chicks scrambled around on the dusty floor of the barn, some of them leaping up onto the edge of the trough and teetering there, then leaping backward excitedly, as if they had faced down danger. I will never forget the color of the juice illuminated by shafts of light between the old boards and stones of the barn walls. Next day, the head man of the village stood in the farm yard by an open fire over which kettles of hot water boiled. He was cleaning an enormous wine barrel, almost as tall as he was, even rolled over on its side. He had put clean stones in the barrel and would pour hot water from the boiling kettle into the barrel, then roll it back and forth so that the stones knocked loose the deposits of sediment from the year before. Occasionally he would roll the barrel over so that water and purple chunks of sediment would empty out one bunghole. Then he would pour more boiling water in and roll the barrel back and forth, shaking the cleansing stones around inside.

I understood then that tending the vine and making the wine were ancient and elemental tasks. I felt that I had breathed the atmosphere of Dionysius. Now, on our own place, Bill and I were eager to be part of the tradition.

In the third year, things started to look up. I was busy with my job, but Bill had put a lot of effort into cultivating the vineyard that year. He had finished putting up poles and stringing wires to support the vines. Then the vines had to be pruned at the end of winter, before bud break. Pruning involves cutting away old growth and leaving two to four canes of growth from the year before. Grapes grow on first-year wood. These canes must be spread and tied to the supporting wires so they can send up their green shoots, forming a sort of harp of vines woven on the wires. Each cane is secured with one or two pieces of plastic tie. As summer comes on, the vines form small green blossoms along the new shoots. If pollination goes well, these later turn into grape clusters that dangle along the wire. The top of the plant forms leaves, which are required for photosynthesis and to ripen the grapes. Other necessary jobs include cultivating around and between the plants to cut down on competition from grass (though we leave the paths between the rows as mowed grass) and trimming away the "suckers," shoots that come up from the roots or from the main stem of the plant and which take away nourishment from the main branches.

The grapes also must be sprayed periodically. In late winter, a dormant oil spray goes on to protect the grapes against overwintering pests. Sulfur sprays to prevent a blight called powdery mildew are essential at frequent intervals during the growing season. Powdery mildew grows on the surface of the grape and, vampire-like, sucks all the moisture from the fruit, leaving a hard, dry husk with no juice to make wine. Bill sprays as little as possible, but in this area powdery mildew can wipe out a grape crop in a matter of days, and spraying is the only way we've been able to control it.

There also is hedging, the process of cutting back excessive vine growth, which can cause the vines to loll and break off. Such excessive growth also is said to give the wine a "cooked asparagus" flavor and may shade the grapes too much for timely ripening. Later in the season, as the grape clusters fill out, it also helps to pull away some of the lower leaves on the plants to get heat and light to the grapes and thus speed up the ripening process and intensify the flavor. All of this is time-consuming, sometimes backbreaking work. In two acres we have approximately fourteen hundred plants. The vines are about six feet apart in rows and the rows are ten feet apart. Many newer vineyards are going for greater density than that. Small European vineyard tractors make it possible to cultivate between narrow rows. We, of course, have gone with what was here when we moved in. Although we bought a small tractor, essential for spraying, much of the work is hand work, plant by plant.

Some of our friends in the valley are working on turning their vineyards into commercial wineries. One family we know, with a smaller overall acreage than we have but a larger planting of grapes, has made a success of commercial production by selling to a local winemaker who sells his highly prized stock on "futures." That is, he takes orders for his wine before it is even bottled and regularly sells out. Our friends distinguished their vineyard early on in the amateur winemakers competition at the state fair. They still make their own excellent pinot noir, but their grapes also go into the vintage of a highly regarded local winery. When we first moved out here, we wondered whether we should be doing something like that, but the first two years were unpromising, and by the time the vines began to produce we realized how much hard work, expense, and time was involved with even a small vineyard. We sold a few grapes to the U-pick market, but then we decided we could not afford to go commercial because it would require a heavy investment of start-up capital and hiring outside workers to help plant additional acreage and to cultivate and pick the grapes. It also would require a lot more chemical involvement to ensure a usable final product.

Moreover, most Oregon vineyards, like ours, are from cuttings on their own roots. Since we moved out here, we've heard a lot about a plant louse called phylloxera, and about vineyards in California that had to be taken out because of it. Phylloxera is native to America. Native American grapes—the wild fox grapes and Concord-type varieties—are immune to phylloxera. Transmitted inadvertently to France in the nineteenth century, phylloxera virtually wiped out French vineyards until they were replanted with French varietals on American phylloxera-immune rootstock.

In spite of this risk, planting with cuttings is the easiest, least expensive way to start a vineyard. You just root small cuttings from older plants. Every vine produces abundant cuttings with the winter's pruning. These cuttings can be rooted in a bed and transplanted the following year, or rooted right in the planned vineyard if there is sufficient moisture to keep them from drying out as they develop roots. But these cuttings from European varieties—that is, the kind of grapes used to produce fine wines—are vulnerable to phylloxera. Now phylloxera has appeared in some Oregon vineyards. As vineyards become infested, they must be replanted with wine varieties on phylloxera-resistant rootstock. Grafted cuttings are far more expensive and time consuming to produce.

Contamination by phylloxera is spread by equipment, workers' boots, and so on, from one vineyard to another. We are relatively isolated from any other vineyard and we don't hire workers to work the vines, so we may be able to avoid phylloxera contamination. Should the vineyard ever show signs of infestation, however, we would have to decide whether to replant with grafted vines.

But even maintaining a two-acre vineyard involves a tremendous expenditure of hard work and attention. Consequently, we decided for the time being to keep our vineyard small and cultivate for home use only. Any one family legally can produce up to 200 gallons of wine per year, which would be plenty, even for our large family. We hoped our vineyard eventually would produce that much.

In the third year, our pinot and chardonnay grapes began to respond to all the work and produced a more substantial crop. It still was far below the desired poundage; nevertheless, we got about seven hundred pounds of chardonnay and a couple hundred of pinot. This was not difficult to harvest by ourselves. We made wine in early October, bottled it in late December, and with great satisfaction started to drink it in January. After all, we told ourselves, the Italians like young wines, and nouveau has a respectable place among the French. We were not exactly in the aged, fine wine business, but making our own wine and sharing it with appreciative friends and relatives—even if the wine was young in the extreme—was a pleasant novelty and a luxury.

It seemed our fourth year would be a turning point. It definitely was going to be a good one. As harvest neared, we kept a nervous, delighted eye on the grapes. "Pinot noir" means black pine cone, from the shape of the clusters and the dark blue color of the grape.

An abundance of the small, blue-black, cone-shaped clusters promised a wealth of wine.

The chardonnays, too, were abundant, even more so than the pinots, and it appeared the harvest would be early. The fall went on and on with one glorious hot day after another. The chardonnays took on a deep golden glow, their early green opacity turning to a transparent yellow fire.

As September passed, Bill tested the sugar in the grapes on a daily basis. We were waiting for the sugar content to show up as twenty-two brix—that is, about ten to eleven percent sugar—in order to produce the best-tasting wine with an alcohol content of about eleven percent. In the process of fermentation, sugar is converted to alcohol. The taste of alcohol is somehow comparable to sweetness on the palate, and yet, as any wine drinker knows, it is not the same as sweetness. Volatile alcohol acts as a vehicle for the complex flavors in wine. Some people stop fermentation by adding sulfites before all the sugar has been converted to alcohol, and thus retain a residual sweetness in the wine—sweet Rieslings in particular are like that. But we wanted a dry wine where all the sugar had been converted to alcohol.

It's hard to predict which day is going to be *the* day. The pinot and the chardonnay vary a bit in ripening, the pinot usually, but not always, coming on first. We planned to pick the pinots ourselves and then call in others for the chardonnays. With our small crop we thought we should be able to pick an acre in one or two days, depending on how many friends and relatives we could attract to the harvest.

It was early October when Bill decreed that the pinot noirs were perfect. He began to pick. I was back teaching by then, but I picked when I came home from work. We had bought a beautiful little barrel press from a company that specializes in cider-making equipment. Its wooden staves were bright new wood, unstained by the grape, but not for long. Before going into the press, the grapes had to be crushed and broken up to start the juice. In the old days, this was where the stomping came in. Later we would buy a used stemmer-crusher, such as wineries use for the initial crush, but early on we had to find other means. We tried plunging our arms into the grapes and breaking them with our hands. This was enough to introduce us to the tingling experience we had heard drives "stompers" into a dancing frenzy, as the skin on our arms began to burn and itch from the acid in the juice, but as a method for crushing it was slow and ineffective. Finally, Bill came up with the solution of using a clean two-by-four to pound the grapes in a bucket and break them up. Then the crushed grapes went into the clean new plastic garbage can, where, for several days, the juice would sit on the stems and skins, beginning to ferment. When chief vintner Bill figured it had drawn enough color and tannin out of the skin and stems of the grapes, we put the pulp into a straining bag and squeezed it with the hand-operated wooden press, a barrel-shaped construction of staves loosely connected by metal straps and mounted over a draining platform on legs. As the press bore down, grape juice ran through a hole in the platform into a bucket. From there it went into glass carboys. We added wine yeast (Montrachet), applied fermentation locks to vent gases while keeping air from getting back into the carboys, and set the wine in a shady place to work.

All this time the chardonnays, which were much more abundant than the pinots, were ripening to a clear gold. We were lucky. The fall rain had not yet begun. It appeared that we could begin to harvest the chardonnays that weekend. We put out the call to relatives and friends. The Saturday of the harvest was bright and hot. Bill, always eager to get to work, already had been out in the vines for a couple of hours when people began to arrive. I had lined up enough scissors and clippers for a dozen people. Grapes must be cut from the vine. Their stems are tough and they usually can't be pulled off without ripping the plant or breaking the cluster. There were small plastic picking buckets to go around.

Intrigued by the novelty of wine harvest, people began to move through the vineyard. The first ones to fill buckets trudged back up the hill from the vineyard with buckets balanced on their heads, dangling from their arms, or clutched protectively to their chests. Bill took over the crushing operation now, with Joe, my brother-in-law, helping. My young niece, Lauren, had come dressed in a full multi-colored skirt and bright blouse. As she picked, she took short breaks to whirl and dance between the rows of vines, her skirt fanning out in a blaze of red, yellow, green, and black. The dogs, Jack and Mollie, tried to distract pickers by dropping rubber balls or sticks at their feet, but everyone was intent on the harvest. Kate, the small daughter of friends, insisted on carrying her own bucket, and meandered along behind her mother, occasionally snipping off a golden clump. Bellen had come from Seattle with college friends. My sisters picked along with their children, Lauren's older sister, Marie, and nephews, Nick and Dylan. Moss, Monica, Stephanie, Alex, and Jon arrived and disappeared into the vineyard. People came and went, picking a row then stopping to rest in the chairs beneath the big oak by the kitchen, drinking wine from last year's harvest and eating cheese and crackers. I put on an Italian opera tape (the same one that our dear-departed hen, Scalpina, had enjoyed), and sounds of Verdi flavored the bright air.

I picked one more row and then went to the house, where I began making pizza from the dough I had put to rise earlier in the day. I spread the dough with tomato sauce from our garden, mozzarella, herbs from the flower bed, and chopped sausage. Soon we were all eating pizza between pickings. Slowly, as the afternoon went on, we picked the entire crop of chardonnays.

We wanted the chardonnay to be a pale straw color. Unlike the pinots, which were left on the skins for a few days to gain color, the chardonnays were crushed and then pressed immediately. After the juice had settled in the large containers, yeast was added and the wine was left to ferment in a shady place on the brick walk outside the kitchen. After about three weeks, the wine would complete its first fermentation and be transferred to carboys and capped with a water-filled fermentation lock. Of course we tasted the fresh juice, trying to guess what kind of wine it would make. In our eager inexperience we were unable to predict whether it would be like "pineapple with a scent of new mown hay" or "spring flowers touched lightly by lemon." We simply hoped it would make very good wine—and how could it not, given the blessing of friends and relatives all joining in the harvest on this beautiful October day? After the harvest we sat around finishing off the pizza, drinking more of last year's wine, eating fruit and cheese and chocolate cake, and glancing now and then at the late sunlight on the rolling foothills of the Coast Range.

Year by year our small vineyard has continued to improve, as has our wine. For the first years, we didn't use oak barrels for aging because they were expensive, and one thing after another had to be bought, replaced, repaired, paid for…but we finally splurged and bought two thirty-gallon barrels at $167 each, one for pinot and one for chardonnay, and this has added the taste of "oak" and "toast" to our productions. It's marvelous. Why didn't we forego the new water heater and buy barrels before? Oh well. Maybe next year we'll add two more. Our barrels are not traditional French oak, which is even more expensive, but are made of oak from Arkansas. Nevertheless, they impart a pleasing extra dimension to the taste of the wine. "Toast," by the way, is the particular flavor added to the wine from the scorching of the inside of the wine barrel staves when the barrels are being made. Flavor from the oak will lessen as the barrels are reused from year to year, but they can be used for several years, and we are thinking of adding another barrel this fall, maybe trying a different kind of oak to see its effect.

As my thoughts run on grapes and wine, I look out at the hills and remember gold at the heart of a stone.

Mud

Mud. The color of February in the country. Mud outside the back door. Mud on the dogs' feet. In the barn, summer gopher holes that came up inside the walls now channel rainwater and create a muddy mess in the rams' side of the barn. There is even a sinkhole at the gate. Oregon has had record rainfalls this winter. The ground is saturated. Every gully and every stump hole fills with water. Slides have plagued all the coast roads. Two miles down the highway, Stiller's Mill road fell into the creek one night, washed out by a week of solid rain. Russell Creek Road, past our place and up the hill, has caved into a ravine, and who knows when it will be fixed? Woodland Loop has a big sinkhole in it.

Mud and manure, the barn in winter. I go out in my nightgown, jacket, and boots to let the sheep out. Ten good lambs so far. No new ones this morning. One stillborn yesterday. What happened there? We can only guess, will never know. Perhaps the ewe didn't get its head cleaned off and it suffocated. Perhaps there was some invisible fault in the making. A dead lamb looks so small. I wondered if something was wrong with it—undersized? early?—but when I picked it up by the hind legs and carried it out to bury it, the lamb felt heavier than I had expected, as long and heavy as the others. It was only its sodden stillness, its wool covered with the gunk of birth clinging like wet mold to the sunken body instead of drying and filling out. The mother still looks bewildered today, wanders around baaing now and then for the lamb she knows she should have. After twenty-four hours, the afterbirth has not come all the way out—another problem. I call the vet to get something for the retained placenta. This is depressing.

Later I go back to the barn to gather the animal feed pans to wash them. Everything is wet, muddy, shit-covered. I spread the plastic basins in the yard and hose them off. It's cold out. The Coast Range is hidden by clouds. More rain expected. The mud sucks at my shoes. Thank God for clogs.

I try to remember the summer drought, as it's called—that time in the Willamette Valley when everything dries out and it never rains, sometimes for as long as June to November, leaving the oaks dusty, turning grass to gold and bare earth to a hot stone. It's a delicious time of year. The grapes ripen as their leaves turn yellow, dry, and part to reveal the thick clumps of fruit. The air tastes like hot apples, and you can smell the honey in the hives heating up from yards away. All day, turkey vultures soar on thermals over the valley. We walk around wearing shorts and skimpy little shirts, bare feet in sandals we can slip off when we sit down to cool our heels. The sheep lounge under the oaks' shade at midday, chewing and digesting. The lambs will be fat, weaned, and well-grown by then, but no one has to go to auction yet. It's too hot and dry even for mosquitoes. Sunsets are peach-colored and late. The crickets start their nighttime music. Of course, if it goes on too long after the grapes have been picked, we all start yearning for rain. Desiring the wet air, the dove-gray sky, the comfort of the fire in a wood stove on a drizzling day.

And now we've had it with rain. And it's mud time. Bill goes by the vet to pick up a shot for the ewe with the dead lamb. The lamb has been buried under the lilacs and its mother seems to have forgotten it. She doesn't care if there's afterbirth hanging on her heels. She grazes far out in the pasture which is, thanks to the abundant rain and mild winter temperatures, green. We'll have to corral her when he comes back to give her the shot, but it will be okay.

Bulging with her unborn lamb, Flora wanders up to the fence and noses around for stray treats. I remember the time Flora had a lamb in the upper oak grove on a rainy winter day a couple of years back. I brought it in out of the weather. She followed me to the barn but then didn't want to get penned because, although she saw her lamb in the barn, she thought, confusedly, maybe it also was still up in the oaks. When I tried to block her in the barn, she charged at the door and banged me in the knees so hard I flew completely off my feet, came down on my back, and knocked my wind out. For a few minutes I wanted to kill her.

Flora's mother is Aurora. Flora is in the "mythic" line along with her older sister, Echo. We also have the "good spirits" line of names (Amity, Harmony, and Eftehia—which means "happiness" in Greek); the "vegetation" line (Clover and Holly); the "sweets" line (Toffee, Fudge, Honey); and another set that I'm not sure what to call, except that it has, for me, a nice attitude (Why, Fancy, and Grace). Every once in a while we throw in a lamb name that doesn't fit a category (like Dagmar or Gloria, or Bela's twins, Elvis and Elton John), but I try to keep the associations because it's part of my record keeping. Besides these associations of meaning derived from their mothers' names, we name the lambs according to the alphabet. This muddy February we're in the J year. That's ten years of keeping sheep.

On a day like this, I think, maybe I shouldn't name anybody this year. It makes it easier. Maybe I should get out of the sheep game altogether. Muck and mud and midnight lambings. Looking for sheepsitters when we want to go out of town. I raised my kids. Do I really need sheep? Tomorrow is Valentine's day. Maybe what I really need is a pot of those big red tulips from Payless. I go back to the barn to check on Amity's lambs. She has twin ewe lambs, born a couple of days ago. Amity is our oldest ewe now, since Why and Toffee died. She had udder damage a couple of years ago, perhaps from over-enthusiastic lambs (lambs butt their mothers' udders to get the milk to come down), so she has milk on only one side. It would be easier if she had just a single lamb, but she almost always has twins. The twins are taking turns nursing, and she seems to have a lot of milk on the one side, so maybe it will be okay. I give them supplementary bottles just in case, at least to get them started.

Amity is white but she often has black lambs. These two black ewe lambs are oddly mismatched in size. One of them is twice the size of the other. She looks a lot like Elvis. The other looks like a sturdy runt, like Amity in black. And she has a high-pitched, insistent baaa, like one of those tippy-toys, which won't let Amity forget her. Waa, waaa, waaaa! She is really little. I worry that the big lamb will get most of the milk, so I go out with a bottle, pick up the runt, and lay her across my knees. A three- or four-inch scrap of umbilical cord dangles from her belly, like a dry little stalk of grass. It'll fall off in a few days. I've got mud on my socks and a dab of sheep shit on my jeans. Outside the dim barn it starts to rain again, but I spread fresh straw right after breakfast and it's nice in here. Through the door I see the Coast Range, purple behind a veil of rain and mist. The lamb drinks well from the bottle, sucking the milk replacer into her triangular little black head. She has an earthy smell, partly the smell of birth, partly wool, partly sheep piss. But it's a nice smell. Her tail wiggles as happy lambs' tails do when they eat. Her black eyes shine. There is a spot of white on her nose. The J year. I think I'll call her Joy.

The Fat-Tail Sheep

Lambing season is over. Everybody's fine. Sixteen ewes have produced twenty lambs. We would have had twenty-one, except for the one that was stillborn. I felt sad at its loss, but overall this was a good lambing year. The lambs were especially robust, large and vigorous, standing up and trying to nurse as soon as they were born, following their mothers, not wandering off and getting lost.

I can see them now from my window, the ewes grazing in the upper pasture under the plum and walnut trees. Almost all of the lambs are grazing now as well—except for the last two, who still are more interested in milk, gamboling, and playing bump-off-the-stump than in eating grass. I am grateful.

I remember one lambing season two years ago that was not so happy. Inexplicably, one disaster seemed to follow another. I won't dwell on all that went wrong, but I do want to tell the story of Toffee, and what happened with Toffee that year.

Toffee was our oldest ewe. When we got her, she was already five years old and had not had a lamb that year. Perhaps she had never had a lamb. We bought her as part of a "starter flock," along with Why, who was three, and the two ewe lambs, Amity and Aurora. Toffee was the only colored sheep in the bunch, but she was an unusually pretty color of grey with a soft black monkey face and black feet. She also was very fat, with a big fat pad on her rump.

One sheep breeder who stopped by thought Toffee must have descended from the fat-tail breeds, which are desert sheep, traditionally raised by the nomadic tribes of Uzbekestan and other rug weavers of Asia. These fat-tail sheep develop great mounds of fat near and in the tail, which serve, like the camel's hump, as reserves for lean times. This fat also has been prized by nomadic tribes for its nutritional richness—a kind of sheep butter.

Oddly, one drawback to this fat deposit is that it may interfere with breeding. I didn't know whether Toffee really had a fat-tail sheep in her lineage, but so far as we knew, she had never had a lamb. We had been told she was a Romney, though not registered, but colored Romneys may owe their color to the reintroduction of older strains into the breed to produce different shades of wool. Once, all sheep were mixed colors of black, gray, and brown. Gradually, in the history of wool production and sheep domestication, light fleeces were selected and the colors were bred out to produce a standard white fleece, attractive in itself and more easily dyed to the desired color than colored fleeces. So perhaps Toffee, with her pretty blue-gray curls, was recapitulating her ancestry in more than one way. And perhaps her fat tail also was interfering with motherhood. Toffee did not produce a lamb, though the rams showed great interest in her at breeding time and she seemed willing.

This went on until Toffee was past her tenth birthday. We decided we liked her for her fleece and character, and gave up expecting a lamb. Then one evening as we were doling out the day's rations in the barn, I realized that Toffee had developed an enormous udder. Her wrinkled, leathery teats were distended and her bag was like a big, pink balloon. Toffee was going to have a lamb. Next morning, she produced a pretty black ewe lamb we named Fudge. As Fudge grew up, she lightened to a warm soft brown.

The next year, Toffee lambed again—a pretty, delicate lamb with a fleece like feathers. Fudge had been tractable, easy to handle, easy-going, as Toffee was. This new lamb had a wild streak. Any handling seemed to throw her into a panic. She could not get used to having shots, having her hooves trimmed, or being sheared. For the most part we tried to avoid handling her in order not to scare her. Her fleece was much fluffier than the usual Romney, and streaked with pretty shades of brown and grey and beige. She also was a very small sheep, with light, thin bones and a pointed muzzle. Nothing about her suggested a fat-tail sheep. She was more like a Shetland, though not that small, but certainly delicate and soft-wooled.

The next year, Toffee had a third lamb, this time a robust black ram. I thought he was one of the most beautiful lambs I had ever seen. He was heavy and chunky, with a thick, lovely fleece and a loose skin that formed wrinkles around his sturdy neck. He was very calm, not at all like his skittish older sister. I loved to pick him up to feel his floppy vigor, his sturdiness, and the pleasant texture of his thick, black fleece. I imagined keeping him as a breeding ram.

One day when the lamb was a few days old, we were gone for a couple of hours and returned to find Toffee baaing. Her lamb was nowhere in sight. We searched the pasture. We searched the woods. We looked up and down the road and into all the thickets to see whether he had gone through a fence. We left Toffee out of the barn that night so she could call him if he had simply gone to sleep in the woods somewhere and would later wake and respond. All night long I returned to the pasture, listening for the tiny baa that would tell me where the lost lamb was. Toffee and I wandered the pasture all night, but no lamb returned to the fold.

We still don't know what happened to that lamb. Did someone steal him from the pasture? Not too many miles from here, there had been sightings of a mountain lion in recent weeks. Had the lamb been snatched by the mountain lion or some other wild animal? Sturdy as he was, he was of course small, just five days old. I thought he was too heavy for a bobcat to drag off without leaving a trail, but perhaps a mountain lion or a coyote could have taken him.

Poor Toffee. For two days she wandered the pasture baaing for her lamb. She inspected the other lambs restlessly, sniffing them, hoping each one was hers, then turning and going on to the next. She was a very good mother and had nurtured both Fudge and her second lamb with all the attention and milk any lamb could ask for. Finally she seemed to give up looking for her lost lamb.

A month later, Toffee's wild-acting delicate daughter had her first lamb. Lambing seemed to throw her into a panic. She would nose the lamb and baaa at it, then jump away and eye us nervously if we came into the barn. She seemed unable to settle down enough to nurse the lamb. This panic activity went on all day. Then, twenty-four hours after delivering the lamb, another sorrow—the wild little ewe collapsed from some mysterious toxicity and died, leaving an orphan lamb. Any animal disaster always leaves me wondering what I might have done to prevent it and with a feeling of mournful helplessness.

Sadly we buried the mother and made up a batch of milk-replacer for the lamb. It drank greedily from the bottle. I fed it at two-hour intervals, and then, before I went to bed, I tucked it into a corner of the barn in a pile of hay with a towel wrapped around a plastic, two-liter pop bottle filled with warm water to keep it snug.

Early in the morning I came out to see whether the lamb had survived its first night without its mother. At first I couldn't find the little lamb in the milling throng of sheep. I opened the door and the sheep filed out into the pasture. Then I saw Toffee, with the little lamb close at her heels. She stopped. The lamb began to nurse.

I couldn't believe it. It had been almost a month since Toffee's own lamb had disappeared. Surely her milk had dried up. Moreover, ewes don't willingly adopt other ewe's lambs. I wondered: Could the lamb really be getting milk from Toffee, or was it just getting comfort? Later I checked Toffee's milk supply. There was a thin stream of milk. As the days went by this milk increased. Toffee seemed to believe she had found her long-lost lamb and the lamb had found its (grand) mother.

Summer went by. The lamb grew fat and healthy. When he was six months old, we sold him with two ewe lambs to some people who wanted to raised sheep for colored wool.

Then it was fall. Toffee was thirteen and a half. Though sheep can live to be older than that, this is getting on for a sheep. Toffee was becoming frail. The effort of raising her daughter's lamb had been strenuous. Her fat tail was no longer so fat, though she had the pasture at her disposal and we gave her all the alfalfa and COB she wanted.

Each day, Toffee spent more time lying down than grazing. One morning in October, she walked out of the barn and lay down in the grass near the watering trough. She crossed her front legs and put her head down on her knees. For a long time she lay there as if she were dreaming in the sunlight. Later in the morning, noticing her still lying this way, I went out to see if she was all right. Her eyes were shut. Toffee had died a peaceful death dozing in the grass in the pasture. I will miss her, but I think she had a good life for a sheep.

Blanket

Bill is making another blanket. It's going to be a plaid twill made of four colors of wool: a creamy white, a taupe gray, a medium cinnamon brown, and a darker brown, which is almost black. The fleeces from which the yarn was made came from Honey, Echo, Happy, and one "Lamb Boy" who went to live on a different farm. They are the natural colors of our sheep. The blanket is going to be a present for one of our children who has just bought her first house.

The wool was shorn from our sheep a year ago, at the end of January, and has gone through several stages of preparation since then, including skirting, washing, picking, carding, and spinning. When the wool was shorn, it already had been growing on the sheep for a year. It was about two months ago, just after Thanksgiving, that Bill began to spin the wool for the blanket. Making a handmade wool blanket is not a fast process.

Today Bill has enough yarn and is beginning to "sley the loom," that is, to thread the warp through the heddles and tie up the harnesses. Bill has an eight-harness loom, which is capable of making a single layer of cloth four feet wide. To make an eight-foot wide fabric, he must weave two levels at the same time, so that the cloth is woven folded down the middle. This complicates things because the weaver can see only the top half as he is weaving, and may miss mistakes. The best thing, of course, is not to make any mistakes.

The heddles are narrow metal bands, each one less than a quarter of an inch wide and a foot long, with an eye in the middle for the yarn to pass through. The heddles, 960 of them, one for each warp thread, are suspended from the eight harnesses. During the weaving, these harnesses are lifted in various combinations by wires attached to the foot pedals, or treadles, and thus the pattern of the weave is determined. Needless to say, there are many different possible patterns and the tie-up is similarly varied. When all 960 warp threads have been tied up and the harnesses linked to the correct treadles, he can begin weaving.

Simultaneously, our shearer has just finished shearing our sheep for another year. It's the beginning of lambing season. In the first week of February, we're past the January cold spells into a stretch of mild weather, and shearing them now before lambing keeps the fleeces in good condition.

The shearer comes from western Australia, near Perth. He has black hair and snappy black eyes, and sounds like Crocodile Dundee. He married an American girl and now lives in the Willamette Valley, but he still makes his living shearing sheep. It's back-breaking work but he makes it look easy, flipping the sheep up on their rear ends and going over them with his electric shears. He rarely nicks one and he has a touch that makes the sheep relax and loll over instead of kicking and fighting. They lean placidly against his knees as he shears. "There you go, girl," he says, releasing the shorn ewe. "Nice and neat and full of lambs." Aurora, veteran of many shearings, gives a shake and saunters out into the field. The sheep seem to enjoy the lightness of putting off a year's growth of wool. Sometimes, after shearing, a ewe will momentarily indulge in a spell of gamboling, as if she were a lamb, leaping up in the air and running back and forth in short bursts of energy across the pasture. It's humorous, like seeing someone's sedate mother get into a pillow fight.

At first, when we had just a few sheep, Bill and I would shear them ourselves, first with a hand clipper that looked like a large, primitive pair of scissors. You can see these new in any farm store, but they actually resemble the tools found at late Iron Age and Roman sites across Europe. Sheep shears have been around for at least two thousand years.

Later we bought an electric shearer that looked like a big-toothed shaver. This was more efficient, but still difficult. I would wrestle the sheep and try to immobilize it while Bill sheared. Even with the electric shears, it took us most of an hour to shear one sheep and we occasionally left "buttonholes," as my father called the scary nicks in the sheeps' soft skins. It was hard on us, hard on the sheep, and the sheep looked funny when they were done, with long and short patches of unevenly clipped wool. Having a professional do the job seemed like a good idea. This year he did our twenty-eight sheep in about three hours. When he finished, they looked great and seemed to know it, frisking around in the cool, clear air.

For a short time after they are sheared each year, the sheep have trouble recognizing one another. The shearer does the rams first, and when they are done they stand outside the barn shouldering each other back and forth like restless high school boys trying to reestablish an equilibrium. Then the rams sniff and investigate the ewes as they emerge, neatly trimmed, from the barn. "Hey, sweetheart, new in town?" seems to be the question.

Though it is an ancient practice, gathering wool by shearing the fleece is the result of human intervention and selective breeding over the centuries. Primitive sheep don't have a solid, continuously growing fleece, but rather a coat consisting of a mixture of coarse hairs and a softer undercoat that is shed annually, like dog hair. Until the invention of sheep shears, people probably harvested wool by plucking it from the sheep or off bushes where it caught during molt.

Recently I have heard about experiments with removing fleeces chemically to cause a break in the wool and thus make it possible to simply peel off the fleece. A break in the wool sometimes happens naturally, when a ewe has been stressed by illness during pregnancy, for example, but in that case the fleece is apt to be ruined.

Hard work as it is, there is something ancient and satisfying in the actual clipping of the wool. The act connects us to the ten thousand years or so of human cultivation of sheep flocks, probably beginning with early efforts to simply track and control a particular wild flock and continuing through centuries of progressive domestication.

I love to see the fresh fleeces rolled inside out, the clean under part of the wool and the true, unweathered color of the fleece revealed. Our white sheep vary from palest cream and snowy white to the traditional off-white or ecru, through all kinds of grays, from a bluish silver through warm taupe and an almost lavender gray, to dark steel grays and warm cinnamon browns. Some of the darkest sheep are virtually black, especially in their younger years (the colored sheep tend to become lighter with each year's fleece), but when the black wool is prepared and spun up with its sunbleached outer tips, it looks more like a bittersweet chocolate brown than a true black. The different sheep also show varieties in "crimp," the wavy or curly character of the wool, as well as in fineness of wool. Some of the fleeces are softly fluffy and others lie out in tiny lustrous crinkles or waves. These variations in color and crimp are beautiful and interesting. Crimp also helps the fleece spin well and gives the finished yarn a bouncy resilience. After the shearing, we bag the fleeces separately to keep the colors and textures distinct.

Commercial wool-buyers don't really want colored fleeces, though Jefferson Woolens, a mill on the east side of the valley, has bought some occasionally. White wool is more in demand, but unless you have a lot of it, from a flock of several hundred, the price, ranging from forty to fifty cents a pound, is insignificant. Imagine—a sheep spends a year growing its fleece. A young ram may have a really large fleece, say twelve to fifteen pounds. Finer fleeces, and therefore softer ones, are naturally lighter. A lamb's first year fleece, wonderfully soft and lustrous, perhaps the best fleece of all, may be only five pounds. Can this beautiful cloud of texture, warmth, and color really be worth only two dollars fifty cents? It costs that much to have the sheep sheared. To earn money from selling wool, one really needs to sell premium fleeces at a higher price to the handspinner's market, and some producers do that by mail order or at fairs and sheep shows.

With our small-scale production, Bill processes the fleeces, spinning what he can into yarn and then weaving it into that rare item, a handspun woolen blanket. What is left we may sell to the commercial producers for whatever we are able to get, in order not to waste what we cannot use and to help cover expenses.

When I was a child, I often slept beneath a green and white blanket that had been made from wool off sheep my father's parents raised long ago in Kansas. It was not exactly a blanket, but rather a length of plaid wool, wide as a bed and twice as long, so that we folded it to use it doubled. It was a twill, with the diagonal texture and give of that weave. The two-color plaid was soft gray-green and creamy white. It had been made on a factory loom, in exchange for wool from the farm, a length of plaid to be used as my grandparents wished. When it passed on to my parents, it often ended up on my bed until I grew up and left it behind. In recent years, my mother has replaced the wool blanket with an electric blanket, and the old blanket, with its worn edges and a ragged hole in the middle, generally rests in a cupboard, but the wool is still beautiful and capable of giving warmth, even though it has been at least sixty years since it adorned the back of a sheep.

Wool is like that—durable and beautiful. In clothing, it will keep the wearer warm even when wet (something I learned when the children were going to outdoor school and we parents were advised what to pack). Wool also is fire-resistant and, unlike some synthetic materials, does not give off toxic gases. It is an amazing fiber.

The blanket Bill is weaving is going to weigh about six pounds. When we shear, the fleeces of our adult sheep weigh between four and ten pounds, depending on the size, age, and character of the animal. Fleeces from our full-grown younger rams may weigh up to fifteen pounds. When the wool has been washed and carded for spinning, it may lose half its weight or more, depending on how oily, dirty, or filled with bits of hay and other material it was when the sheep were sheared. Before washing the wool, we pick out bits of hay and seeds, manure tags, and twigs picked up in twelve months of browsing. Heavily weathered and particularly dirty parts, such as belly wool and the manure tags on the hind legs, are removed entirely. This "trash wool" is not wasted—we use it to mulch the fruit trees, where it eventually decays and releases its protein and minerals to the ground. The cleaner part of the fleece is then washed. We do this ourselves, several months after the shearing, in the hottest days of summer, one fleece at a time, by soaking a fleece in the washing machine in hot water with a full cup of detergent. It takes all day to do a fleece. First the fleece is soaked with the detergent for an hour. Then the washer is drained (without agitation, which would shrink and felt the wool) and filled again with clear water. We repeat this process as many as four or five times, for about half an hour each soak, until the rinse water seems relatively clean. It's just as well not to remove all of the grease, though if the wool is too greasy (full of lanolin and oil from the sheep's body), the grease will clog the carding machine. We then carry the clean fleece outside and spread it carefully on the back deck, where warm summer air will dry it quickly.

We used to try to wash fleeces in winter and dry them indoors, but it took days for them to dry—even when spread and ventilated on a hammock strung out in front of the wood stove. Now we simply wait for the hottest, driest days of summer, in late July or August, in order to do the drying outdoors. As the fleece dries, I can't resist stopping from time to time throughout the day to pick at the beautiful fibers, carding them apart with my fingers, turning the wool so that the air can dry all of it evenly. As the fleece dries and is picked this way, more fine bits of old hay or grass still in the wool will fall to the sheet and can be shaken away. When the drying is done, the wool will be puffy and cloud-like from picking, but it will still have the wonderful lanolin and wool smell of a homewashed fleece.

After the wool is washed and dried, it usually is carded before spinning. Most of the time, but not always, we send the wool out to be carded and turned into "roving." The carding machines have rollers covered with sharp metal picks that comb the wool so the fibers all run more or less in the same direction and can easily be spun into a strong, fine thread. Bill sometimes cards the wool himself with a small hand carder or with two carding combs, but for large amounts of wool such as he uses in blankets it's a welcome economy of time to have it done by machine and returned to us in medicine ball-sized globes, each one unwinding in a thick, continuous ribbon of carded wool or roving, ready to be spun.

After the wool has been carded, it takes Bill six to eight weeks to spin enough wool for a blanket—not working every minute of every day, but as many hours as anyone could spin without developing a severe cramp, sometimes as long as three hours in a day. When the wool has been spun in a single weight thread, he plies the yarn, that is, respins it, but this time, instead of spinning from carded wool he runs two strands of the single-strand yarn through the spinning wheel so as to twist the two strands together into a two-ply thread.

I have grown accustomed to the singing sound of the wheel; it is a pleasant, busy sound. Sometimes he works on the old fashioned wheel, a Louët, which requires a steady pumping with one foot to operate, but more often, these days, he works on the electric Ashford wheel. Years of spinning take a toll on the muscles of the foot and the electric wheel provides a break from that.

Anthropologists speculate that early people must have noticed sheep's wool caught and twisted on bushes and how it formed long strands that could be woven, like the reeds and grasses and bark fibers they used in making baskets, into a useful fabric. The use of hides as blankets or clothing came before wool weaving, but a woven fabric would be lighter and softer. Imagine wearing a garment made of a wool-backed hide to keep warm instead of a sweater or a worsted blazer. Moreover, used for wool instead of hides, the animals themselves are not sacrificed. An established herd would have been a source of wealth in early times, and the owners would have been unwilling to kill their livestock unless it was absolutely necessary for food.

Weaving is a complicated and painstaking process. Pattern is not self-evident. Sequences must be followed. Threads break. Mistakes compound themselves. Understandably, Bill has great appreciation for the history of spinning and weaving, as well as for the unknown prehistoric men or women who first practiced it. When we visited the Victoria and Albert Museum in London a while back, he was fascinated by the textile collection, which ranged from plain cloth to medieval tapestries. Medieval weavers created complicated jacquards using floor looms with an intricate arrangement of pedals and other moving parts. Even the rigid or tapestry loom can be used to make high art out of a utilitarian craft, as in the beautiful works of Navajo rug weavers we saw recently at a show in San Diego.

Bill works on an eight harness jack loom, a Macomber. Twill, the weave he is using for this new blanket, is basic but extremely beautiful and useful. The weave produces a pattern of diagonal parallel lines, quite apart from the color pattern of the blanket, which is going to be a squarely designed plaid. That is, there is a texture pattern in the fabric apart from the color pattern. A twill produces fabric with an appealing give and drape. It is soft and flexible but durable. The fine diagonal ribbing, barely visible unless one is looking for it, nevertheless adds thickness and strength to the fabric.

The blanket is growing on the loom. I can see the pattern of the plaid he has worked out as he finishes the second repeat. This blanket, made from wool that already had been growing on our sheep for a year when it was shorn from their backs a year ago, is meant to be an heirloom, a sign of eternal values, an object in which beauty, tradition, and utility come together as is rarely possible in the modern world. It's also intended to be a comfy spot. This blanket will last a lifetime if treated with minimal care and kept from moths and the agitation of modern washing machines—probably the two main enemies of handwovens. A year in growing the wool. Another year in which the wool was, at appropriate and convenient times, sheared, skirted, picked and cleaned, washed, dried, teased, carded, spun, plied, washed again and dried on a "woolly winder" to make it into manageable skeins, threaded onto the loom and tied up according to the predetermined pattern to be used, then woven into the final fabric.

Bill does not sign his weavings, though I sometimes have urged him to attach a signed label. He is a modest man whose modesty hides a kind of pride in the ethos of the handweaver as a craftsperson—someone anonymously carrying on centuries of accumulated learning and skill. I reflect that I am too egotistical for this, but I understand his viewpoint.

The week is going by. The blanket continues to grow on the loom. Bill sits on a wooden bench he made himself, padded with a small blanket he also made himself years ago, when his initial experiments in spinning and weaving involved working with a drop spindle, basically a weighted stick, and weaving on a crude frame he had made from two-by-fours. The yarn in this small, old blanket is a thick single-strand, not even plied. It looks almost as if it has been woven with locks of wool straight from the sheep, and is a warm white, the color of old ivory. The yarn he is using in the new blanket is much finer and, because it has been plied, stronger, but both objects have their own beauty and integrity.

Bill weaves in his stockinged feet. His hands move the shuttle back and forth as his feet work the loom treadles in varying order to create the pattern. He is a man who says he doesn't dance, but there is a kind of dance in the quick movement of feet in the weaving pattern. When I hear him occasionally muttering to himself, I know that a thread has broken and must be repaired or he has made some small error that must be undone and corrected, but that doesn't happen often. He listens to music as he weaves, especially classical cello music. There is something similar, I think, in the interweavings of Bach, Beethoven, Corelli, and the movements of the loom. And there is some connection, also, between the music, the weaving, and the currents of time. The blanket grows in time and weaves together the strands of human history, almost as if the spirit of some man or woman two thousand years ago has been carried, unbroken, into the present.

Finally the blanket is done. He cuts if off the loom, leaving a foot or so of spare threads that he will discard into a paper sack where he keeps leftovers for mulching a fruit tree or stuffing a pillowcase for a cat bed. Yarn scraps actually can be reprocessed, snipped up and recarded, or used in the process known as garnetting, where bits of another color of yarn are carded into a main color to add accent spots.

The finished blanket is huge. Spread on a bed, it drapes out across the edges and onto the floor for a foot on each side. But after Bill has knotted the ends into a fringe, he will soak the blanket and size it. He agitates it briefly in warm water in the washing machine, not enough to spoil the fabric but just enough to tighten the weave. Then he stretches it over an arrangement of poles in the front room where the wood stove is burning warmly. Here it will dry for a day or two. When he takes it down and tries it again, it fits the queen-sized bed perfectly.

When the blanket is dry, he folds it and puts it into a well-sealed plastic bag and puts the whole thing into the deep freezer. There it will stay for a few days in the unlikely case any moth eggs have survived the whole process. Freezing will kill such pests. Normally there is no problem with moths in a blanket unless it is stored in a dark closet without any covering or moth balls. In our experience, a blanket used in the light and on a regular basis will not develop moth attacks.

The finished blanket weighs just under six pounds—fairly heavy for a blanket, but it is large. Figuring the amount of yarn it took to make it, Bill and I came up with the following figures:

The warp required 7,680 yards of single-spun yarn, or 3,840 yards of plied (doubled) yarn. The weft—the part that is woven back and forth through the warp—required 6,144 yards of single-spun yarn or 3,074 of plied yarn. (Because of the way the yarn is tied on, there is a certain amount of waste on the fringe ends of the warp, and thus the warp thread is longer.) The single strand of handspun yarn required to make the blanket, wool from about one-and-a-half fleeces, is approximately 7.85 miles long.

It is also about the length of human history.

How Smart are Sheep?

One indication of the intelligence of sheep is that they do not really like people. They can't help it, and it must be in their own best interest because evolution seems to have wired it into their brains. I don't mean that sheep are openly hostile—certainly, pet sheep can even seem friendly—but overall, a sheep's orientation is away from the human race.

I've been reading about it. Tests on sheep show that different parts of their brains act up when they see different figures—specifically, other sheep they know, sheep of their own breed, sheep with big horns, dogs, and people. The activity the sheep's brain exhibits when it sees a dog and a human being shows that it thinks human beings and dogs are more alike than sheep and dogs or sheep and people. Of course, from a distance, if a human being gets down on all fours, there is a little uncertainty and the sheep's brain may start sending "possible other sheep" signals until the sheep gets close enough to realize its mistake. Then a sheep might think you're a dog, until you stand up. By and large, from a sheep's viewpoint, dogs and people fall into the category of trouble.

One researcher, noticing this similarity of response to dogs and people, concluded that sheep have emotions. If you're around them much, it becomes obvious that sheep have emotions, so this is no surprise, but it's interesting to see how research proves it. According to the researcher, if a sheep were merely responding to appearance, a dog, with its long muzzle, might elicit a response that would associate the dog with a sheep. But instead, the brain waves elicited by a dog are close to those elicited by human beings, and thus we know that the sheep is experiencing an emotional response to both of us, dog and person, and that response is not thrilled.

Of course, if we are carrying a big grain bucket, the brain waves are something different. But in any case, it surely can be called an emotion—that is, a particular brain response that readies the sensate animal for some sort of action, fight or flight or pig out. My sheep always look pretty happy when the human-brings-feed image impresses itself on the optic nerve and thence to the brain.

I have run into people who don't believe that animals feel emotions ("have feelings" is the way they usually put it). This is probably just a way of rationalizing what we human beings do or have done to animals, the meaning of emotion being coded into the word "feelings." If a creature has no feelings, it can feel no pain. But sheep do have emotions and feelings, however they may vary from our own.

It's true, sheep do not run to the fence in friendly curiosity when they see a person. To a sheep, a human being is almost always something to have as little to do with as possible, unless that human being is bearing alfalfa, COB, or Fatena, or preparing to open the gate into a new browsing area. Bummer lambs raised with a bottle are a dramatic exception, but they are confused by their upbringing. A bummer (a bottle-fed lamb that has been orphaned, or whose mother is unable to raise it for some reason), will see you coming or hear your voice across the pasture and come running, baaing its head off with that charming, ringing, baby baa. They'll crawl through the smallest hole in a fence, run to you, and begin butting the back of your ankles, looking for an udder and waiting for your milk to come down. It's hard not to feel loved by a sheep when this happens.

But as you wean them they become less attached, maybe even resentful after a while—another emotion. I've seen weaned bummers use a kind of body language that can only be called sulking. They plant themselves in front of you, but when you don't produce a bottle they turn and pretend to be looking at something invisible on the ground. And if they continue their fence-hopping and escape tactics, and you end up chasing them back into the pasture, after a while they get downright suspicious and will stay away from you. In the sheep's brain, sometimes you're just the thing that's standing between them and the all-you-can-eat salad bar in the kitchen garden. You're Trouble. Just the sight of you (not to mention your dog) sets off wary brain waves in the sheep.

Of course sheep have other brain waves too. Horns on sheep are signs of status, of a possibly challenging big honcho sheep, or of a sexually mature, hot-to-trot ram. Scientists have tested sheep by showing them pictures of sheep with horns, and have found that the bigger the horns, the more excitable the brain waves become. These were simple line drawings—horn porn for girl sheep. The scientists performed this test only on horned breeds. I haven't been able to find out whether hornless breeds also get turned on by big horns, but they do react positively to familiar sheep. As one study put it, "Sheep know who their friends are." That's why they get negative vibes when they look at people and dogs.

One curious thing about the way a sheep's brain reacts to different faces is that a sheep doesn't recognize its friends upside down. Though a sheep will react with familiar brain waves even to a crude drawing of a sheep right side up, if you turn that picture upside down the sheep's reaction is something like, "Whaa....?"

Supposedly, arboreal primates recognize other arboreal primates right side up *and* upside down. That's because they hang from trees, sometimes upside down. But you almost never will see a live sheep upside down, and never of its own free will. Sheep don't even roll over on their backs for the fun of it, as horses do. They don't roll over to scratch their backs like dogs or cats, or loll around on their backs at the beach like people on vacation. At the most, a lying-down sheep will stretch out its neck on the ground or lounge to one side, but sheep are very upright creatures.

In fact, a sheep on its back is liable to be in trouble. Our old sheep Toffee was rather fat, and once in a while, especially in rainy weather when she hadn't been sheared all winter and her wool was heavy and wet, she might lie down on a hillside and then accidentally roll over on her back. She then was unable to roll down a quarter-turn more to her other side and get back on her feet, and she certainly couldn't roll uphill, so she would lie there till we found her and rolled her over so she could get up. As she lay there, on the slope of the hill, you can imagine, being upside down, she'd see us coming and think, "Who *are* those creatures?"

With tricks like these, sheep often have been equated with stupidity, mainly because of their herding instincts, which can be so strong as to get them into trouble, such as a whole flock jumping off a cliff because the sheep in the lead goes over first. (We've never heard of human beings doing anything like that, have we?) But really, most of the time a sheep knows what a sheep needs to know.

One researcher tried to measure sheep intelligence by conducting a test that required the sheep to remove a black cloth from a box to get at feed—a test that horses and cows already had passed after varying numbers of attempts. The sheep confronted with this enigma stamped its feet, as sheep do when confronted with danger, urinated, as they do when nervous and stymied, and generally didn't get the idea until after fifty-five tries, putting them, according to this tester, below horses and cattle in intelligence.

But another test showed that sheep could learn to recognize and avoid noxious plants after only one bad experience, and that was something they had to figure out after eating a large variety of plants during the same browsing period, and with feedback (that is, a bad reaction to the noxious plant) coming as long as several hours after the plant was consumed. This is an example of single-trial learning when it comes to something a sheep needs to know. Other tests showed similar results, such as when lambs who saw their mothers eating an unfamiliar feed immediately learned to eat that feed too. Lambs normally would take a while to discover that something unfamiliar was good to eat. In further testing, researchers found that the sheep still relied on this learned information years later, even if they hadn't encountered that feed in the meantime. This indicated that lambs learn what to eat by watching what their mothers eat, and they learn it quickly.

I will not make claims that sheep are especially intelligent in human terms, but obviously they do know what they need to know to be sheep. Our older ewes are the ones who have learned which gates they can jiggle to sometimes escape the pasture when they want to. Amity, Aurora, and Bela all have learned how to lie down and crawl under a woven wire fence if there is the slightest slack in the wire, much to our inconvenience. Now it seems clear that their lambs also are learning this behavior, while other younger mothers and their lambs can't figure it out.

The sheep also know when to go in at night and how to sort themselves out. At sundown, our rams go to a pen on one side of the barn and the ewes go to the other. We just close the gates. We had a small ram born late last year that we kept to put a little more size on him. We let the lambs, male or female, go in to the ewes' side. This small ram continued to go in with the ewes and to hang on to his lamb status all through the winter. When this year's lambing started, and the ewes' side was getting crowded, we decided he needed to go into the rams' side at night. It took three nights of chasing him in there from the ewes' side. After that, he consistently went to the rams' side on his own.

Susan M. Oullette, writing about sheep in seventeenth-century America, says that although sheep in Ipswich, Massachusetts, were individually owned, during the day they were taken out to the village commons by a sheepherder hired by the community. This collectively managed flock of sheep, known as the "Great Herd," was brought home at night, with the various groups of sheep turning off to their owners' places. The essay doesn't say whether the sheep turned off on their own, knowing they were home, or whether the shepherd cut them out of the flock as appropriate. My guess is that the sheep, like our ewes and rams, would have known where their own home barn was.

Sheep know what they need to know.

This past year we had personal experience with an eight-month-old ram trying to find his way home. I like to think it's also an indicator that sheep are smarter than some people think. We sold the ram lamb to some people who live about twelve miles from here, on the other side of a wooded ridge and up their own hill. To get to their house, you have to drive north about six miles, then turn off and double back, driving down a twisting road through a narrow valley between two big ridges. Then you turn off and drive up a narrow road that passes through some other people's woods, and finally out into a clearing where their ranch is.

The week after we sold the lamb, a neighbor on the opposite side of the highway called to ask if we'd lost a lamb. She'd found one that looked like ours—a black Romney. I said, no, all my lambs were accounted for. After I got off the phone I began to wonder whether the recent buyers of the lamb had made it home with their acquisition. I called. The buyer said, ruefully, the lamb was missing. They'd brought him home and unloaded him into a pen by himself because the ewes were in another field down the road. Seeing no other sheep and panicked by the trip in the horse trailer, the lamb jumped the fence and took off. Sheep don't like to be alone, especially if they've been raised with a lot of other sheep, as ours have. If there is one instinct above all others in sheep, it's the herding instinct. The lamb would have been perfectly happy to stay where he was, had they unloaded him in with the ewes right away. They had, after all, purchased him to be the sole sultan of his own harem. But so far as he could tell, after they put him in the strange truck and drove him all that way, they'd put him in isolation. It scared the heck out of him. A healthy, well-grown lamb can jump a lot higher than most people think if his adrenaline is up. This guy cleared the fence like Superlamb and took off.

When I told her about the stray lamb that had turned up in our neighborhood, she got excited and said they'd go look at him right away. Of course it turned out to be the lost lamb who had been wandering for four days and finally turned up on the sheep farm across the highway, about six miles through thickly wooded countryside and over the mountain from where he'd leaped the fence. He'd clearly been headed in the right direction.

Whether it was all by chance or not, we'll never know. Wild sheep, and sheep raised on vast ranches or downs, need to find their way. Do even small-farm domestic sheep have a strong directional sense? How would it operate considering the ram lamb had been taken to his new home via winding country roads, not at all the shortest path cross-country? How had he managed to strike off through the woods and end up that close to where he had been born? Did he know what he was doing, or was it just an accident? It wasn't exactly *Lassie Come Home*, but it was interesting.

This time when the new owners returned the lamb to their farm, they made sure there were a couple of ewes waiting for him in the pen. He took one look and was immediately happy to settle down. Sheep, after all, know what they need to know.

Paws

About 2 a.m. the thunder and lightning started, one of those storms at the end of the summer when the season doesn't know which way it's going. I would have slept through it except that Jack poked me in the arm with his rubbery black nose. He hates loud noises. As the storm came closer, his poking became more insistent, though I rolled over and covered my head, trying to ignore him. Pretty soon he was tapping my shoulder with a paw. What did he want me to do, turn the thunder and lightning off?

I rolled onto my back, patting his head, then put a hand over one of his ears, trying to diminish the sound of thunder. He took this as an invitation to climb onto the bed and soon was leaning his fifty-five pounds of trembling weight on my chest. I moved to the center of the bed, away from him. He followed me. I crowded over to Bill's side of the bed, thinking perhaps I could sleep with a dog in the bed because I was just too tired to get up and do anything about it. But in a few minutes I realized I couldn't sleep with Jack breathing on my head. His fear of the storm made him pant rapidly and violently, and his breath had a nervous, sweaty odor.

Bill was awake by now. "Down, Jack. Down!" he muttered from beneath the covers. I pushed Jack off the bed and tried to get him to lie on the floor, his usual sleeping location. This only made him panic more. He tried to claw his way into my armpit.

I sat up in bed as Bill got up and led Jack out of the bedroom, shutting the door. We had just started to doze off when, at the next rumble, there was a wild clawing sound at the bedroom door, which flew open. Jack bounded for the middle of the bed, between us.

I seriously considered getting up and going somewhere else to sleep, as I often had done when the children were small and too many of them would wake and climb in beside me during the night. But this was the dog, for Pete's sake. He was supposed to be standing guard over the pack. I should have gotten some tranquilizers from the vet the last time this happened.

I pushed Jack off the bed and onto the floor once again, scratched his stomach, rubbed his head, spoke to him in soothing tones. He lay on the floor, trembling, but quieter. He put his head down with a thump. Mollie turned restlessly under the bed, her sleeping place. I could tell she was getting irritated. Loud noises didn't bother her a bit, but Jack acting up did. Any moment she was likely to dash out from under the bed and bite his ears, her usual treatment when he acted silly. Mollie was definitely a border collie princess.

Jack seemed to be settling down and I almost dozed off when there was another crash of thunder and Jack leaped onto the bed, landing on my shoulder with his sharp toenails extended.

Bill got up again and turned on the light. Jack looked apologetic, but Bill took him by the collar and led him to the back room. I felt apprehensive (it reminded me of the scene in *Peter Pan* where Mr. Darling puts Nana in the yard), but I couldn't spend the night with a dog sitting on my head and I had to go to work in the morning. I hoped that the storm would pass soon and we could all get a good night's rest.

In the morning I woke to Bill's anxious face. "He's gone," he said. "He broke out a window and he's gone." I couldn't believe it. He had been safe where he was, but dog reasoning is not the same as human reasoning. He had thought he could outrun the thunder.

I knew that in the past when Jack had been frightened by a nearby gunshot or a storm he would take off for the upper woods. Usually we found him by driving down the road and up the neighbor's driveway on the other side of the woods. Calling him, we would entice him out of the woods, or, if he was feeling canny, our calling on the other side of the woods would sending him running back home to greet us at the back door, as if to say he'd been there all along…where had we been? I walked the length of the property in my nightgown, calling into the dense fir woods, but Jack did not appear. Mollie followed me, and as I called she howled. I knew she thought I was howling too, calling the pack together, so I appreciated her effort. We walked the fence line once more, howling for Jack. No luck.

I had to go to work so I showered and went off with a heavy heart, leaving the search to Bill. It was a nice morning, wet after the storm, but sunny and clean looking, as if the world had been purified. I didn't want to believe we would lose Jack. He was ten years old, but instead of getting used to occasional gun shots and thunder he was more fearful than he had ever been. Mentally I formed one of those prayer-like thoughts out of childhood—if I can only have my dog back, I promise to get him some tranquilizers. Bill said he would call the dog control as soon as they opened and he would drive around looking.

All day at work, whenever the phone rang, I expected to hear Bill's voice announcing news of Jack, for good or ill. I braced myself. I knew there were people with livestock who would shoot any stray dog they saw crossing their property. It wasn't until about three in the afternoon that he called. "Good news," he said. "He was up on Russell Creek Road a couple of miles, almost at the washout. Something told me to take one more drive around and I went up that way. I drove around the curve and there he was, in the middle of the road, coming down the mountain. I think he was finding his way home. He looks pretty worn out. He jumped right in the car, like he was glad for the ride."

That evening Jack slept like a sailor home from the sea. Mollie looked at him suspiciously from time to time and sniffed his sleeping form as if to see where he'd been.

Years ago I had another border collie who was gun shy, MacHeath. He spent every fourth of July hiding and trembling in the shower stall. Mollie, on the other hand, doesn't seem bothered by noises at all. I wonder if it's genetic or if it has to do with some early exposure. Personality in dogs is certainly as sharply delineated as in people, although, as is probably true of both, it may arise from some genetic predisposition as well as from training and the company they keep. From years of living with Jack and Mollie we've come to know their individual behaviors, but that doesn't mean we understand them.

One of Jack's quirks has to do with sticks. Any long pole or long-handled tool sends some almost uncontrollable urge through his body. He wants to circle and grab. If someone picks up a broom or a shovel, he starts racing around like a maniac, looking for a chance to bite the thing. He doesn't look angry when he does this; on the contrary, his face, his whole body, express delight. This is not desirable behavior, of course, particularly if he sees someone with a cane or on crutches in a public place. I wonder if this is the odd expression of some instinct bred into him over centuries of selecting for herding traits in British border collies—say, a reaction to the herdsman's long crook reaching out to snag a sheep—because it is such a powerful and automatic impulse. But I have to face it: we are not expert herd dog trainers, and whatever we were supposed to do to turn this inconvenient trait into a fine and useful thing, apparently neither Bill nor I was genetically or educationally prepared to do.

At one point when Jack was a half-grown pup, I tried to teach him to jump over a pole instead of chasing it. Jack's father, Craig, was a superior fence-jumper, and when Craig's trainer directed him to a pen full of sheep he would run up the cross bars of the fence and leap right over, dancing across the backs of the milling sheep. I'd been impressed. But when I first directed Jack to jump over a stick I held out, as preparation for greater and later jumping, he looked embarrassed, uncertain. He would begin to jump and then pull back, as if he could not believe what I was asking him to do. I held the stick out with one hand and beckoned him over it with the other. Finally he gathered his puppy muscles and leaped, then gently but definitely bit the arm I was waving. Fortunately I was wearing a heavy jacket. He looked foolish after that and ran up to me wriggling and fawning as if he wasn't sure what to expect. Somehow I was giving him the wrong message: "Jump over this stick and bite my waving arm." I'm happy to say that in spite of my training, Jack eventually developed the ability to jump fences on his own without an arm to bite on the other side.

I also tried to teach the dogs herding commands. "Come by" is the command given border collies to tell them to circle a flock clockwise, to gather the sheep into a tight circle before moving them. The first time I called out "Come by" to Jack, I was amazed. He began to run in a clockwise circle around the sheep! I was amazed because he had been only a few weeks old when we'd gotten him and hadn't had any training yet. This was too easy, I thought. He obviously loved it and began to run faster and faster. His circle became wider and wilder. He ran as if he'd forgotten the sheep, had forgotten me. His tongue hung out as he ran and ran. I thought he was going to fly off the ground.

I tried to go on to the next step, to get him to "stand" and "walk up." But he kept circling. The sheep stared at him. *What next, you idiot pup?* they seemed to ask. Jack just kept running. "Stand!" I yelled one more time. He skidded to a stop and threw himself on the ground, panting. He had obviously had a wonderful time. The sheep continued to stare. Then one of the ewes took off for the barn and the others went after her. No doubt that was some accomplishment.

Mollie, in the meantime, was upset by the loudness of my commands and had taken off for the house. She would have none of it.

After many such episodes, during which I felt that my training abilities were no match for Jack's boisterous instincts or Mollie's delicate sensibility, they both learned to "Put the sheep away" and both loved to be called on for this duty. Or perhaps it was just that they realized what I was trying to do, in my botched human way, and so they did what they had been born knowing how to do. They also learned to sit and roll over and shake hands, not exactly sheep-herding skills, but it was easy enough to teach them these tricks. For herding, it seems they have all the right instincts but I don't. Sheep herding, after all, is based on the sheep's fear and the dog's hunting instincts. I soon realized I didn't like to see the sheep frightened. Except in emergencies—say, a sheep getting over the fence into the road or through a loose gate into the yard—I didn't send the dogs in. The sheep themselves soon became trained anyway. As the sun went down they would return to the barn, and in the case of a rare truancy, all it took was for me to say loudly, "Put the sheep back, Jack. Put the sheep back, Mollie." Hearing me call the dogs, any errant sheep would turn and run back where it belonged, whether the dogs gave chase or not.

I still like to go to sheep trials and watch the trainers and their dogs, trained to perform complicated maneuvers at whistles or hand signals. But we are comfortable as we are, without the competition.

With their breeding and intelligence, Mollie and Jack do have great language skills. It's obvious they listen to what we say and they understand a great deal of human language. Border collies are said to have large vocabularies; they understand, perhaps, hundreds of words we people use. I'm sure it's only their physical inability to form words aloud that keeps them from talking with us. A word such as "bath" sends Mollie to hide under the bed until she is sure it's your bath and not hers you're talking about. "Treat" on the other hand brings her out of hiding. "Toast" also is an attractive word for the dogs, as they enjoy getting the last bite of our breakfast toast in the morning (what we call, only half-facetiously, "the dog's due"). "Squirrel" sends both of them rocketing out the screen door, without so much as a hand gesture toward the walnut grove. We also can ask them to find one another. "Where's Barbara?" or "Where's Bill?" gets an immediate response. "Into the truck" is one they like, since they always enjoy a ride to town. A joking, friendly "Hi!" as if greeting guests will send them barking to the driveway whether there's anyone there or not. Of course there are all the commands: "Sit," "Lie down," "Go in the bedroom and leave company alone," which they understand and act on. Jack also hides if he hears the word "mosquito," because it might mean that Bill will slap an invading insect with the newspaper, and this bothers Jack's gun-shy nature.

More mysterious, perhaps, is the way they communicate to us. When it's time to feed the sheep and close up the barn at night, Mollie is apt to come into the living room, where we are watching television or reading, and stare at Bill with a fixed stare that he calls "waving." Bill says, "She's waving me. Guess it's time to put the sheep in." And it is. Jack, on the other hand, is particularly eloquent when he's hungry. He communicates this fact by bringing his dish and dropping it at my feet. If I don't notice, he is apt to pick it up again and rap it lightly against my shins. He also does this when he already has food in his dish but likes the smell of something we're cooking—bacon, for example, or baked chicken. Training visitors to throw a ball is something they both specialize in. No sooner have visitors arrived than the dogs have cunningly placed a ball within their reach and stepped back to stare at the trainee's face with fixed attention. Yes, they are "waving" company. And it works. Time after time, I have seen the unsuspecting one, as if hypnotized and without even interrupting the conversation, pick up and throw the slobbery ball one of the dogs has brought.

I admire dogs in general. I love the way they look, with their varied ears and coats and builds, each one speaking of some long genetic history, but I particularly find border collies beautiful. The border collie usually is black with white markings or sometimes sable or blue merle. They can be either smooth or rough-coated. Jack is smooth, and his coarse, shining hair sheds water like a seal's. Mollie is a more old-fashioned-looking border collie, smaller, with a plumy tail and haunches and a soft undercoat. In the past, border collies have not been listed in the AKC registry because they never have been bred for conformity to body type. Rather, they have been bred for intelligence, and it is their intelligent faces and the language of their expressive bodies I love so much: the dark, alert eyes, the long muzzles, the rubbery black noses alert for every scent, and especially their soft, expressive ears, standing up so as to be able to take in sounds and signals, but slightly flopped over at the soft tip, shedding the winter rains of upland sheep farms and wintry marshes, turning this way and that with exquisite attention.

Border collies can be painfully sensitive and still be good workers. My parents often talked about Fanny, the dog on our farm in Kansas, where I was born. She would take herding commands from anyone, but my grandmother, Grace, was the only one she would deal with in the house. When she wasn't working, Fanny retired to a spot behind my grandmother's chair and no one messed with her. "Soft" border collies like this get their feelings hurt if you raise your voice. You might as well save your breath. Mollie is like that. Jack, on the other hand, except for being shy of loud noises, is the original goodtime border collie, rough and ready as they come.

Though they are different in appearance and behavior, and came from different breeders, oddly enough, Jack and Mollie have a common ancestor. When we studied their registration papers, we found among the various names of their predecessors that each was related to a great-great grandfather, "Sweep," who lived, like some of my own ancestors, in Scotland. It's interesting to scan the names on these papers: Phil, Cap, Topsy, Tip, Queen, Leck, Drift, Tarn, Bosworth Coon, Rusty, Cookie, Mirk... There is a whiff of aristocracy, a tinge of the hearty common.

Aristocrat or not, Mollie will hide when she sees preparations for a bath. Jack will grab a towel in his teeth and jump into the tub. Mollie sleeps under the bed at night, but in the morning, when we have our coffee in bed and read the paper, she climbs out from underneath and gets up to nap on the foot of the bed. Jack would never dare, and she wouldn't let him. When she sees we've finished our coffee, she politely gets down and the day begins.

I'm happy and relieved that Jack has returned. He seems to have recovered from the previous stormy night and nudges me in a chummy way. He wants his head scratched. Besides, I'm putting on my shoes and maybe that means I'm going for a walk. I scratch his smooth head, feeling the hard bone beneath, moving my hands around his ears. When I put my hand down, he noses it and flips it back on top of his head—the hand juggler. He is so alert, it seems his alertness flows out from his head into every muscle, into his long back, into his tense, runner's legs. Everything in him is focused on running, on rounding up. I think: more of his brain is in his four paws than mine. Then I remember. Too bad, I don't have paws.

Deer Creek, Wet Prairie

Sometimes I try to imagine what our farm was like back before it was a farm, before anyone cultivated it, planted it, tore up its natural ground cover, grazed it, and built on it. I was told it had been an old peach farm, but I wonder about that because there are a lot of wild plums in the hedges, and peaches don't grow that well here. Our place isn't prime farmland, and as far as I can tell it hasn't been tiled for drainage.

The soil maps put us at about three hundred feet above sea level and describe the natural growth as oak savanna characterized by Oregon white oak, wild rose, grassland, and poison oak. In some of the lower wet areas are rushes, a little camas, and a couple of ash trees. Along the fencelines and in the woods, besides the wild roses, are fawn lilies, brodiaea, white hyacinth, and mallows, and in some places, particularly where the run-off from winter rain collects and channels downhill, the dark purple, blue-eyed grass, or *Sisyrinchium*, a small, delicate member of the iris family.

In low-lying areas a few miles from our place is enough marsh to imagine this area before white settlement when the fields had not been tiled, ditched, and drained, the water courses not channeled and diked. The onion fields just north of us must have been a vast, shallow, winter lake with all kinds of ducks, geese, swans, and other water-loving birds wintering over. Even now, in winter, when the onion fields flood, flocks of tundra swans and Canada geese feed and rest there.

I learned some things from reading Aldo Leopold's *A Sand County Almanac* about looking at the modern rural landscape with an eye for what must have been once. So I was interested to learn that there is a small remnant of early Oregon wet prairie not far to the south of us. I visited the area with my friend and colleague, Kareen Sturgeon, a botanist actively involved in environmental research and restoration. Some of her students were working on a research project involving twenty-three acres of an old farm that had been donated to the county as a potential park or preserve because it was too wet for agriculture. I went there expecting to see a kind of museum of natural history in a field. My untrained eye could not distinguish what was special about the place, though I was glad for an excuse to get out-of-doors and poke around. It was late October and the wildflowers were merely dry brown stalks. Moreover, the acreage had been overrun with teasels, an invasive, non-native plant. I saw that the land had not been untouched by development, but I knew it was judged original enough to be of interest and work was going on to restore it. I wanted to learn what it was that made this place a remnant of something original, hoping thereby to better understand the history of our own farm and the surrounding countryside.

Deer Creek wet prairie is off the main highway on the way to the coast. Surrounded by hills, it already was in shadow when we arrived around 4:30 that afternoon, about a week after the change from daylight savings time back to Western standard. I gave a last look at the sunlight decking the Coast Range foothills in a golden light and plunged into the tall growth of grass and teasels where a chill seemed to lie across the landscape.

I knew the teasels were a pest, but I couldn't help admiring their skeletal forms and remembered that they have long been used to tease the nap on wool fabric, making it soft and warm. Though this year's stems and flowers were dry and dead by the time we visited, I could see the rosettes of new plants beneath the tangle of fall wreckage. The leaves resembled primrose plants, crinkled and green. Next year, the rosettes would send up the blooming stage of the teasel, a hardy biennial, difficult to eradicate once it has gotten a start.

I made my way to the middle of the field and scanned the horizon. Where I had come from was the ash swale and the car park. Beyond that and all around were hills—golden hills, some covered with pasture land, some with a mix of dark green firs and maples turning color.

I closed my eyes and heard the warning calls of wrens in the thickets, far off car sounds, and, to the west, something like a dog or coyote yipping. The field smelled earthy, a good, dark dirt smell. I heard a pheasant call, and opened my eyes to see three male pheasants flying out of the grass and taking off toward a distant hedgerow, clacking their strange metallic warning cries as they went.

The teasels dominated the field, but I set off to try to identify other, perhaps native, plants. There were some fragile brown stems I thought must be fireweed, now just curlicues of dried fiber with a bit of down stuck here and there. There was something yellow, like tansy, but it was fading so I wasn't sure. There were also thistles, rushes, and bunch grass. Once in a while I came to a clearer spot where the teasel, for some reason, had not spread, and occasional brambles of blackberry vine, another non-native, threatened to take over. On the hill opposite the park were small fir trees planted in rows, and beyond that some old apple trees. Further on, I saw a line of yellow poplars marking the edge of a farm, and a barn in the hills.

Again I closed my eyes and listened. As I did so, I noticed that although I imagined myself to be standing perfectly still, I achieved my balance by swaying slightly, rocking back and forth on the heel and ball of each foot with such minimal movement that someone looking at me probably would not notice. I also realized I was tensing my hand on a bit of foliage I had picked and tried to identify—the fireweed. I loosened my grip and the scrap of vegetation fell away. My hands relaxed and dangled at my sides. The air moved on my cheek.

I looked around. The teasels were swaying, so there must have been a wind, but it was so light I wouldn't have noticed it had I not been paying close attention. So still and yet everything was in motion. It was getting colder by the minute. Now the light was almost off the hills. If not for cars, this place would have been far from where we had started—fifteen miles or so from the college. I imagined walking that far on a late October afternoon, out into a wild countryside, long ago. I wandered on across the field. Here and there I saw small blue plastic flags on wires, from the plant survey being done as part of the restoration proposal. I passed through a patch of warm air and stopped to look around to see why it was there. It was a relatively clear spot, no teasels, not much vegetation, and the wet ground that showed through was muddy and dark. Perhaps a contour to the land was funneling the warm air, the way I feel the layers of temperature when I walk down the lower pasture into the ravine at home. There were some more dry, brown flowers here I didn't recognize.

Further on I saw the dead stalks of asters and some patches of lupine. The lupine seed pods still clung to the stalk, but they were twisted open and empty. I knew lupine was significant at this site— specifically the Kincaid's lupine, the host plant for the Fender's Blue butterfly, which once was thought extinct but recently was rediscovered in the valley and is a candidate for the federal endangered species list. Though the presence of Kincaid's lupine is encouraging to botanists and lepidopterists alike, the Fender's Blue requires at least forty acres to sustain a population, and this area was too small. I wasn't sure whether the lupine I'd found was the Kincaid's or a different, more common variety. I also saw something that looked like a goldenrod stalk, but I didn't know if goldenrod grew in this area. It reminded me of the fields of goldenrod at the end of summer in Michigan, where I'd lived for a while. I saw some daisies and that brown shaggy plant we always called tobacco weed. There also was a twist of vetch mixed with the rest—hard to recognize the plants when they were just dry brown threads and wispy shreds of themselves. I didn't see any remains of Queen Anne's Lace, an introduced and extremely common plant in this area, till I got to the far fence. And yet, even from these sparse clues, I could see that in spring and summer this field must be full of wildflowers.

The moon was up now, half a moon, white as death's bones, and I remembered, it was Halloween. I was chilling. My nose was cold as a dog's nose but my sense of smell seemed acute. The oak near the fence smelled sweet, or perhaps it was the ground underneath it. When I picked up a single leaf and smelled it, not much was there. Maybe the wild rose brambles climbing the fence and dangling in the tree still had some sweet smell. There was another tree, deciduous, no leaves, but full of hanging gray-green lichens. I thought that the fence posts must be really old. They looked rotten but were hard when I scratched them with a fingernail. Lichens and mosses were growing on them. Maybe they were made of oak. They were so blackened with age I couldn't see what the grain was like, but it must have been a long time since anyone had fenced this place off, hoping to turn it into pasture or a crop.

I cleared my nose as Mollie does, and took another whiff. She does that out in the field, blowing air out of her pointed border collie nose and tossing her muzzle, then going back to sniffing whatever interests her. Was that a faint smell of skunk? But then it was gone, must have been something on the air coming down from the hills. A smallish woodpecker flew over, rowing the air with its wings.

It was getting dark. Time to go back to town. I was hoping to see an owl—it was about that time of night—but no luck. I started back across the field toward the path and the car. Interesting that benign neglect had yielded this little remnant of wet prairie. I mentioned that it was surprising it hadn't been tiled, and Kareen said that from the air it appears the land once was drained, but the drain tiles had collapsed and somehow it still retained its character. Now that restoration has begun, it will be interesting to see what flourishes here.

My sketchy observations were those of an amateur. It was not until I talked more with Kareen about the place and read her student Nikole Matthiesen's thesis that I better understood what it was that defined an original wet prairie—specifically, the wet condition of the ground and the nature of the plants that grow there. It had been over thirty years since anyone had tried to farm this piece of land, but those early farming efforts had disturbed the land and made way for invasive, non-native plants. In spite of the invasive plants that included the obvious teasels, blackberries, and wild carrot or Queen Anne's lace, and in spite of the early attempts by settlers to drain and farm the place, enough of the original conditions remained to sustain certain original plants such as tufted hairgrass, or *Deschampsia cespitosa*, which once dominated as much as four hundred thousand acres of the Willamette Valley, before it was settled and farmed. Nowadays many of those acres are used to grow non-native sod grasses, used in lawns and for golf courses, as well as other agricultural products. Though it no longer is found in the great quantities in which it once existed, the tufted hair grass in the principal indicator plant species for the Willamette Valley wet prairie. According to Nikole Matthiesen's information, "The presence of *Deschampsia cespitosa* at the Deer Creek Wetland makes the 23 acre piece of land the largest remnant wet prairie site in the lower Willamette Valley." The Kincaid's lupine, which I later learned grew on the upland portion of the landscape and was not the lupine I encountered, is another survivor.

Wetlands are of interest, of course, simply because they are. But in human terms they also are compelling because they play such an important role in the management of water, pollutants (natural and manmade), and nutritional resources. They act as filters and storage, slowing runoff from storms, extracting nutrients that can flow too quickly into lakes and other bodies of water, unbalancing the ecosystem and causing killing blooms of algae. Because they sometimes have been associated with dankness and gloom, difficulty of access, rank smells, and disease-carrying insects, wetlands have not been appreciated fully in the past, and a major effort of settlement in wild areas has been to get rid of them. Where I lived for a while in rural Michigan, I was surrounded by beautiful marshes and deserted farms. Over the sixteen years or so that I lived there, I saw most of those marshes drained and filled for suburban development.

I'm glad that I grew up with lots of wild spots around and had a chance to explore the woods, pastures, and rivers of Oregon, when it was wilder than now, but even then, in the forties and fifties, the character of the land had changed drastically from the days before white settlement when natural fires, or those set periodically by the Kalapuyan Indians of the valley, suppressed the succession of large woody plants and sustained the grasslands which supplied wild food and an open landscape for hunting.

It's not always easy to know what you're looking at in the landscape. Not long ago, I would have looked at this patch of grass and teasels, which is the Deer Creek wet prairie, and not recognized its character at all. It's good to have the twenty-three acres, even though that is not enough for the rare Fender's Blue butterfly.

When I'm driving to work now, I find myself looking at odd brushy spots in a landscape dominated mainly by farms, wondering just what I'm seeing. Here and there a farmer will take his tractor, year after year, around a low-lying patch of ground, too wet to plow, leaving a tiny remnant of wildness, and some old fencelines, out in the county where the margins of roads aren't mowed, leave a generous "long acre" of wild flowers and brush. My visit to Deer Creek sent me back to our own farm with new curiosity, new eyes, as I looked for signs of what it must have been before it was used for grazing and orchards.

I know that overall our place is not a wetland—quite the opposite—but I think about the brushy low area, on the east side, where water collects all winter and where the land looks black and damp even in summer. I realize there is a small patch of lupine near there, just above the open spot where the camas grows, and the anomaly of the two ash trees in that same area now presents itself as a clue to some wetland character. In vain I look for unusual grasses, but the sheep have been that way and what is left is desiccated and nondescript.

Once I counted sixteen different kinds of grass in our walnut grove, none of which I could identify. Now I promise myself, the following spring and summer I will make an effort to learn the grasses. I will explore that tangled area beyond the fence. I promise myself I will learn to see more clearly what is there, maybe even what was once there, a long time ago.

Peace at Heart

Now that we have been on the farm for ten years, I look back and wonder at how casually we made the move, as if there were no perils at all, as if we knew what we were doing.

We didn't need to leave the city. Things were going well. I was in my forties, three years into a second marriage. I had the college teaching job I wanted and a handsome, loving husband who was patient, sensible, and creative. He was teaching in an interesting alternative public high school. Our kids were doing well. We lived in a big comfortable 1920's house in an exciting neighborhood in the city.

Still, even the happiest person knows that life is often sad. Like a purple thread in a white shawl, sadness pulls the eye into itself. There were nights I couldn't sleep. White nights. *Les nuits blanches.* You turn off the lights but the light stays on.

On one of these nights, at the end of summer, as a hot east wind poured into the valley, I was lying fidgety in bed trying to quit consciousness when, through the open window, I heard a frail, mournful voice calling: *"Help me."* Then it called again. I went outside but could see no one. I walked to the curb and peered up and down the dark street. No one. The call was not repeated. The city was quiet except for far-off sounds of traffic. Someone's Siamese cat wearing a green bejeweled collar stared at me from the lawn, then darted into the bushes. I called 911. A police car appeared and circled the block but found no one.

I returned to bed and dozed briefly, then woke with a sad feeling I couldn't justify. "Help me." I wasn't even sure whether it had been a man's or woman's voice. Trying not to wake anyone, I pulled on shorts and a T-shirt and went to sit on the dark porch. The wind was hot and silky, palpable, a wind from eastern Oregon's high desert. Pouring through the gap in the Cascade Mountains that is the Columbia Gorge, it moved downriver, through the dark streets of Portland, across the west hills, out into the Tualatin Valley and toward the sea.

The movement of air against my skin suggested something physical yet indifferent, like the movements of fingerling trout against your legs in a mountain stream. I remembered floating in such streams as a child, looking down into water pierced by green and golden bars of light, and doing the "dead man's float," lying face down in a creek and watching the minnows nose my arms or tug at my drifting hair. This was like that.

It was three a.m., the hour of sorrowful hearts. The hour of second thoughts. The hour of the foraging opossum and the raccoon. I listened again for the call. "Help me." But I heard nothing. As I sat there, I imagined that the wind was full of swimming ghost fish. Dry leaves fluttered and cast fish-like shadows in the light from the street lamp.

The longer I sat there feeling the wind's passage, the more I was drawn into my fantasy. I felt the flutter of fins on my forehead, tails fluttering along my bare arms. The city was quiet except for the sound of spirit fish swimming to sea. In Ireland, the Gaelic name for wind—Sidhe (pronounced "shee")—also is the name for the fairy people that ride the winds. In Oregon, our winds could well be streams of air ridden by ghost fish: the Chinook, the Steelhead, the Rainbow.

Bill and I had hiked in the Coast Range that weekend, following an attractive trail uphill through dense trees, only to find, after a quarter of a mile, acres of clear-cut land and a group of teenaged boys riding motorcycles up and down the eroded logging road. I felt angry and disgusted. Then one of the boys grinned and waved, looking not like a delinquent and monster, but like someone's little brother. As Pogo said, "We have met the enemy and he is us." By nature, most wild animals hide themselves from us human beings with our stinking machines and self-centered habits. What if the natural world somehow withdrew and left us in a world populated only by human beings in a manufactured landscape? "Help me." Heat lightning crackled over the mountains to the east, but in the city it didn't rain.

The screen door opened. "Is everything all right?" Bill whispered, stepping out into the dark.

"I was thinking about salmon," I said. "When I was little, when the fall rains came, there were so many in the river. I remember seeing them up above Bonneville so thick you couldn't walk across without stepping on them."

"I remember that."

He sat in the chair next to me. After a pause he said, "Maybe we should move down the valley." He knew what I was thinking. It was almost time for school to start. I wasn't looking forward to the long daily drive. I was teaching at a small private college about forty miles south of Portland. It took me an hour each way—two hours a day spent driving. I liked my job, but I didn't like the long commute. There was something deadly about spending all that time in a car.

"We could look at places, just for fun. We wouldn't have to actually do anything this year," I murmured. Seven of our eight kids were using the house as home base out of a variety of needs. Five of them were in college and came home only during vacations, or lived there part of the time and attended college in the city. Two still were in high school, but it wouldn't be long before they were all out of the house, either in college or on their own.

School started. I began my daily drive, one hour each way, and settled into a work routine that didn't allow for nights spent swimming with ghost salmon. The first twenty minutes of my commute were always the worst. Leaving our quiet city neighborhood, I would enter the freeway by way of a long ramp that hurled me into four lanes of traffic moving at top speed. I felt like an astronaut struggling to escape the earth's atmosphere. Or perhaps a fish in a dam-clogged stream. "Help me."

It was my fourth year of commuting. By Christmas break, I was fed up with the drive—and the school year was only half over. I like looking at land, whether I'm buying or not. There's something engaging about going to a new place and fantasizing living there, making it home. Some properties are enticing and stir the imagination toward a new locus, a new life. Some are terrible disappointments, nothing at all like their descriptions in the realtor's big book.

"Just for the fun of it," we began to explore the Willamette Valley for something closer to work that looked like home. We visited a five-acre piece with a stream, no house. The owner pointed us vaguely in the direction of a faint trail and said we could walk it on our own. The land turned out to be on the northern side of a mountain, an almost vertical, wildly overgrown site, with a plunging stream down the middle, and undergrowth of almost pure poison oak. It was beautiful and appealed to my child-adventurer side, as we scrambled down the mountain with brambles in our faces, heavy moss signaling the dankness of that northern exposure. At the bottom of the ravine where the land appeared to clear out slightly we came upon the startling sight of someone's hunting camp. A dozen rabbit skins were tacked to dry on rough boards, and the discarded rabbit heads were piled nearby under a patch of sword fern. The place could have been beautiful, with a Frank Lloyd Wright house perched on its rough slopes overlooking the ravine; it was beautiful in itself, in fact, but there was no grazing land, no sun, and the poison oak, the incline, and the rabbit heads, like some ill omen, put us off. I broke out with a blistering case of poison oak a day or so later.

And so we went from place to place, finding a nice old farmhouse at the bottom of a trash-filled gully, a beautiful piece of land with a beat-up mobile home and a derelict metal barn, an attractive riverside house and ten-acre pasture with a view of a steel-rolling mill, and so on. Always, in our price range, some crucial fault.

On one of these forays to see a different place we passed a tangled spot where the "For Sale" sign was so overgrown we barely noticed it. We stopped, backed up, peered through the bushes. Far back from the road and through a screen of oaks we saw a modest white house, an old red barn, an overgrown pasture. We didn't drive in, but I copied down the realtor's name and number from the weathered sign. The place was ideally situated, about twenty minutes from my job via a pleasant country road, and still not more than forty miles from the city.

Of course the place turned out to be for sale because it had so many problems, at least half of which didn't come to light until we'd lived there a while. The owners had paid too much at inflated interest and had neither the will nor the cash to deal with it all. The wife hated living in the country and declared, mournfully, she just wanted to live somewhere she could walk to a mall with the baby stroller. We wandered through waist-high pasture grass and gazed at the rolling foothills and the blue profile of the Coast Range to the west. A grove of ancient oak trees shaded the little house. Another slope led down through an overgrown, barely started vineyard to hedges of wild rose and blackberry vines, apple trees, and plum trees. Seeing all of this, we said: *this is glorious.*

We hadn't really meant to buy a place for a while, but somehow there we were filling out loan forms. The bank looked at the place and didn't agree on the price of its glory, but we kept at it and came up with a larger down payment. The owners agreed to sell for considerably less than they had paid, and finally the loan was approved. In July, we found ourselves moving in. We decided we would scale back so that Bill could quit teaching and work on the place. "Three years," we told ourselves. "We'll have it all fixed up in three years."

Ten years later, I'm almost afraid to itemize what we've done, all that we've spent, putting in a new foundation, a new septic system, a reservoir for the well, two new barns, new siding for the house, fencing—it goes on.

The house was an amateur's exercise, a poorly planned box to which various other boxes had been attached over its fifty-plus years of existence. We were about to become the most recent amateurs. The "vineyard" consisted of the two acres of rooted cuttings the previous owner had abandoned to blackberry vines. The red barn was so picturesque it would fall down in a windstorm three years after we moved to the place. No doubt we were out of our minds, but clearly we were buying not only house and land but light and angles and vista, sunrise over Chehalem Ridge and sunset over the Coast Range. The oaks were magnificent. Even the oak that fell on our car one winter and totally demolished it, along with two other cars in the driveway, was magnificent for a while.

Sometimes I have misgivings, thinking about our house in the city. I'd like that house on this piece of land. Sometimes I wonder, with all the repairs and work we've done on this place, perhaps we should have torn the house down and built a new one to start with. But the process reminds me of an old movie with Tarzan and Jane swinging vine to vine—you can't look too far ahead, but when you reach for the next handhold, thank God it's there. Money that went into making the necessary improvements seemed to come when it was needed—teaching an extra class, getting a good royalty payment, Bill's unexpected small inheritance, my share of another house sold in a long-delayed payment of a divorce settlement, a tax refund. And when it didn't come, we didn't spend it. It would have been difficult to convince any bank, based on our visible income, that providence would treat us this well, but step by step, things improved.

Having lived here for ten magical years I feel it is time to take account. Ten years. More than enough time for all the cells in the human body to regenerate—which means I'm not the same woman who moved out here. What wakes me in the night is not a call for help but the yipping of coyotes or an almost telepathic awareness of a ewe delivering a lamb. Besides the openness, the landscape and the light, one of the happiest aspects of living in the country has been the animals—even the fox who stole one of our chickens last year. In the city, charted by private lawns and laced by the predatory tracks of automobiles, animals don't really belong. Cats get along in the city, but it's hard to clean up after dogs and they really need more exercise. Poultry is forbidden, particularly noisy roosters. Goats, sheep, and other barnyard animals also are forbidden, even if you have enough space to graze one or two. Even raising bees is against the law in the city, though of course city people expect their fruit to be pollinated. In the city, wildlife exists in the form of finches at garden feeders, or raccoons and possums snitching cat food or garbage off the back porch, but clearly a life connected to animals is not the reason people live in cities. People live in cities to be near lots of people. "Help me."

In the country it's different. Where we live, an elk herd wanders across the hills and deer pass through our yard daily. One of the first things we did when we bought the Lilac Hill farm was to get a dog. Then we got another. Jack and Mollie. Two, it seemed, was the right number.

I don't remember the sheep or the border collie we left behind when I was two and my parents said good-bye to Kansas. I remember only the western end of the trip—palm trees in California, the Oregon surf, a mountain stream with tiny fish in it. Nevertheless, some old imprinted desire has been telling me for years I not only wanted dogs, I wanted to raise sheep. We bought three ewes and a ram and started our flock.

Because the disenchanted previous owners left their chickens behind, we found a surplus of good brown eggs. My daughter and I made our trip into the hills and bought the starter hive from the venerable beekeeper. I raised the geese, who then raised eight goslings. Bill cleared the blackberry brambles and found the vineyard still alive. He nursed it into recovery and three years later we were making wonderful wine. We struggled with drought, a fallen barn, and the problems of a poorly built house. We spent summer and autumn evenings with our chairs lined up facing west, sipping our own pinot noir, as if the sunset in the Coast Range were a splendidly arranged show just for our benefit. We cut rough trails through the woods, to better be able to appreciate the spring fawn lilies, the bright, leathery green and olive-tinted winter growths of lungwort on the trunks of the scrub oaks, the banks of sword fern and wild geranium. A meadowlark sings in our walnut grove all spring. Mourning doves coo in the upper woods and the red tail hawks return. Swans and Canada geese winter in the area, and some mornings we awake to find them in passage, skimming the air just above the house, filling the mists with their ancient cries.

I still drive to work every day, but it's a short drive. The way I go is a slow, winding country road with a pleasant rural character. I pass several plant nurseries and go through two tiny towns with extravagantly expressed "Welcome" signs. When we first moved out here, a series of Burma Shave-style signs along the highway complained in forced meter about the lack of attention to this road from the state highway department. "When asked about potholes, the state's head it did scratch; their only answer, just one more patch." All but one of the signs have fallen into the brush over the years, leaving the enigmatic line, "it did scratch." Someone recently tacked up another sign nearby, "Believe on the Lord," and it makes an odd juxtaposition. Farther down the road, someone else has "brown eggs, 75 cents per doz." Someone else parks a pickup full of scrap wood by the road with a sign: "Free kinlin." However they are expressed, these are signs of life.

At no time do I have to change lanes and often I have the road to myself, although during planting and harvest I allow time for getting stuck behind some plodding piece of farm machinery.

A major change that has come with my country life is the company of animals. It's fun. Someone recently asked me, in a spirit of contemplation, what *is* fun? They were responding to an ad on television about something that was supposed to be big fun— driving your four-wheel-drive pickup at high speed through mud on a mountain, or drinking beer with six guys in a rowboat. Whatever it was, it wasn't my idea of fun, so I wasn't paying much attention, but I did think about the idea of fun. When you're a child, there are prospects that delight so much you can't wait for them to happen: opening Christmas presents, going to camp, having a birthday party. Those are fun. As an adult, I sometimes have those same explosively happy feelings about certain events (returning to visit Greece after thirty years, for instance), but much of the time, adult happiness is a calmer business. Visiting with friends, hiking at Cape Blanco, reading a new Patrick O'Brian novel, listening to our CD of Elly Amling singing Schubert lieder, finding that the St. Cecelia rose has bloomed—these are all things that make me happy. I think of particular moments, such as the feeling of the dog's head lying across my lap as he persuades me by telepathy and subtle pressure to go out and take a walk through the woods. These things are deeply satisfying, but somehow the word "fun" seems too much like nervous excitement to describe adult happiness.

What is happiness? That's a more difficult question. Am I happy? If happiness is the deep down sense of doing what is right, of being in the right place, of going to sleep at night with some confidence that you will wake up in the morning to a world in which nothing too immediate has gone wrong, the feeling that your work is satisfying and worthwhile, that those you love are similarly okay, and that beauty is all around you, then I am surely happy. But I am going to try to pinpoint a particular time when happiness, when peace is the crux of the moment, when well-being is so intense and beautiful that one wants nothing more except to share the feeling with the world.

Many, of course, will find my idea of happiness dull and perplexing, but I am going to try to describe it, a moment of pure happiness which belongs to this place, to this life I am leading here.

I love shaking wild apples down for the sheep in the fall. In October, their wool has grown out from their February shearing. The pasture grass is dry after months of hot weather and the sheep enjoy the juicy wild apples, beautiful in their varied shapes, sizes, and colors, some of them sweet, some of them so bitter I'm amazed that the sheep gobble them so fast.

I go into the pasture. It is the first day of September. The air smells smoky from a field burn somewhere down the valley. The pasture is a pale wheat color but it is only straw, the leftovers of the sheep's grazing. This is the end of a typical Oregon summer and we haven't had rain for weeks. The sheep nibble dry grass, little tufts of green in the shady spots, and the leaves of underbrush. We supplement their grazing with alfalfa and grain, but they like fresh stuff if they can find it. When the rain starts, the grass will green up again. The mild winters of the Willamette Valley encourage green pastures, often even in January. I am of a divided mind, loving the hot hazy days of late summer but looking forward to damp, fresh air. Rain is forecast for this weekend, and all up and down the valley, farmers are anticipating the moisture by plowing and planting the winter wheat. Dust rises in clouds over the rolling farmland.

I go down the pasture and call the sheep. I call by loudly singing out "Sheep, sheep, sheep...." in chanting tones I learned from church when I was a child. They know what this means and come streaming from all directions—twenty-eight of them, for we still have some of this year's lambs—out of the woods, from the lower pasture, from the barn where they have been scrounging for alfalfa stems left in the feeder from the night before. As they come, they start to baa in answer to my calling. I go to a broad, low-growing, wild tree at the bottom of the ravine. Its branches are packed with small, yellow apples the size of golf balls, thousands of them. I grab a branch and shake. Apples rain down and bounce into the dry cavity of the winter pond. The sheep start to run and then they are all around me, gray, black, brown, white, crunching up the apples.

I walk on to the next tree. The apples here are dark red, with a stark white meat. I taste one. Pretty good, but there are plenty to go around. I shake a branch and apples tumble. I duck back out of the way and sheep rush forward to crunch the best ones. I walk on and up the hill. This tree is covered with purplish-pink, small apples on wire-like stems, some wild variation on a crab apple, and this tree too is loaded. I taste one—unbelievably sour! But like lemon juice, fresh and clean. I shake a branch. Some of the sheep are sticking with the earlier choices, but many of the lambs and a few of the mothers rush up. They like these small apples. They can get their mouths around them.

It is getting late, almost dusk. The bright apples glow in the late evening light. I go on to a tree filled with large, crisp, green apples. Good for pies and sauce. I'll save them for us, but to comfort the small band of sheep still following me, I toss down a dozen or so. They pick up the apples with their soft, mobile lips and tip their heads back to get a grip. As they crush the apples with their strong back teeth, the juice foams and runs back out of the corners of their mouths. They look so pleased, I go on, from tree to tree, tasting and shaking down apples. Another tree full of red apples looks promising, but the fruit is bitter beyond belief. I shake it anyway. The sheep eat more. Crunch, snuffle, crunch.

They are excited by this whole process. Now that many of them have had their fill, they just run along for the excitement, nosing the apples and then leaving them to follow me to the next tree. I shake branches full of apples the color of ripe bananas, dusty rose apples, russet apples, and yellow apples with red stripes.

A group of sheep breaks off and forms a loose line going back up the hill. The mountains are purple now—the light makes a golden halo behind them. Where the sun goes down, the sky is red. The sheep's wool takes on a lavender cast from the cooling light as they follow the path up the hill to the barn. They feel the darkness coming and they go toward the barnyard light. A couple of the rams, enormous woolly animals with big, black palooka faces, nudge my hands and turn their chins up for more apples. I shake down some that are red-orange. There are plums too, wild relatives of the hazy blue Italian prunes growing closer to the house. The rams toss the plums in their mouths and spit out the seeds. Once in a while one will crunch up the pits. Their mouths foam with fruit juice.

The sheep. The light. The good, deep smells of oily wool, crushed apples, and drying grass. The dogs snuffling the hedge where they flushed a pheasant earlier today. The chickens settling on their roost in the henhouse. An owl drops out of the woods and soars across the pasture. The cats trill their greetings and twine around the pasture fence posts. The warm light beckons from the barn on the hill. Being in it, with it. This is happiness. There is beauty everywhere and for the moment I am part of it.

References

⊗

Although this book is based more on experience than research, I happily and necessarily turn to my shelf of references when I need help in understanding or dealing with what I experience. Following are my most often used reference books and other works I have consulted in writing some of these essays.

Paula Simmons' *Raising Sheep the Modern Way* (Charlotte, Vermont: Garden Way Publishing, 1976) has been a bedside companion and emergency mainstay during my apprenticeship in the ways of sheep. Other woolly readings that have provided me with hours of entertainment and edification include every issue of the *Black Sheep Newsletter* (25455 NW Dixie Mtn Rd. Scappoose, OR 97056); J. Elliot and J.M. Williams's beautifully illustrated *British Sheep and Wool* (Bradford, West Yorkshire, England: The British Wool Marketing Board, 1990); *Black Sheep Newsletter Companion: Writings for the Shepherd and Handspinner, The First Five Years* (Eugene, Oregon: Black Sheep Press, 1983, edited by Sachiye Jones); and *Colored Sheep and Wool, Exploring Their Beauty and Function* (Ashland, Oregon: Black Sheep Press, 1989, edited by Ken Erskine).

Two standbys on our shelf for checking the fine points of viticulture and winemaking are Philip M. Wagner's *Grapes into Wine* (New York: Alfred A. Knopf, 1976), and the *Oregon Winegrape Grower's Guide* (Portland: Oregon Winegrower's Association, 1983).

The *Oregon Wine* newspaper (published by Oregon Wine Press, Portland) also is a source of news and information about Oregon wine production. Some of my descriptors for wine in "Wine" were quoted from the *Wine Spectator*, an enjoyable source of vicarious high living in the world of fine wines.

My household references on beekeeping were Roger M. Griffith's and Enoch Tompkins's *Practical Beekeeping* (Pownal, Vermont: Story Publishing, 1988), and Walter T Kelley's down-home standby, *How to Keep Bees and Sell Honey* (Clarkson, Kentucky: The Walter T. Kelley Co., 1973).

Although I came to Dave Holderread's book a little late in the goose game, and wished I'd had it earlier, I found his reference, *The Book of Geese, a Complete Guide to Raising the Home Flock* (Corvallis, Oregon: Hen House Publications, 1981), a fascinating and useful guide to tending the flock. I would recommend that anyone interested in raising geese read this first.

Nikole Mattheisen's senior honors thesis, *Deer Creek County Park: curriculum resources for middle school students learning about wetlands and wetland plants* (on file in the Linfield College Library, McMinnville, Oregon), is a clear and useful source of information on Willamette Valley wetlands and the plants and characteristics of the Deer Creek area. The document contains suggested lessons for middle school students as well as a catalogue of plants with their descriptions and background information.

Finally, though I have not drawn directly from these, the following books are almost as frequently brought out in the middle of mealtimes at our house as on hikes, as we seek to identify and learn about a newly spotted neighborhood plant, bird, or other creature:

Daniel Mathews's *Cascade-Olympic Natural History, A Trailside Reference* (Raven Editions, in conjunction with the Portland Audubon Society, 1988), does not deal with our specific area, but there are many overlappings, and the breadth of this reference, evidenced in the table of contents which lists conifers, grasses, birds, fungi, geology, insects, flowering trees, amphibians, mammals, and several other categories of interest, along with the book's color photos and black-and-white drawings, all in a relatively compact form, makes it an essential guide book. Although it is intended for the wilderness hiker, it provides much information and many clues related to marginal rural spaces in the Willamette Valley and Oregon Coast Range as well.

Another favorite, smaller guide dealing with a different region contingent on ours is Charles Yocom's and Ray Dasmann's *Pacific Coastal Wildlife Region*, revised edition (Healdsburg, California: Naturegraph Co., 1965).

As amateur plant-spotters and bird-watchers, we almost always have *The Audubon Society Field Guides* near at hand, particularly *The Audubon Society Field Guide to North American Wildflowers* (New York: Knopf, 1979) and *The Audubon Society Field Guide to North American Birds* (New York: Knopf, 1977).

Additionally, several articles contributed to my understanding of the behavior and history of sheep in "How Smart Are Sheep?" and "Blanket." They are: "A Rush of Maternal Feelings to the Brain" (*New Scientist* 30 December, 1988: 34); "Sheep Know Who Their Friends Are" (*New Scientist* 21 May, 1987: 32); Hutson, Geoffrey, "So Who's Being Woolly Minded Now?" (*New Scientist* 12 November, 1994: 52–53); Kendrick, Dr. Keith, "Through a Sheep's Eye" (*New Scientist* 12 May, 1990: 62–65); Lawrence, Alistair B., "Mother-daughter and Peer Relationships of Scottish Hill Sheep" (*Animal Behavior* 39 [1990]: 481–86); Ouellette, Susan M., "Divine Providence and Collective Endeavor: Sheep Production in Early Massachusetts" (*The New England Quarterly* September 1996: 355–80); Ryder, Michael, "The Evolution of the Fleece" (*Scientific American* vol. 256. 1987: 112–19).